Playground Poets

Let your creativity flow...

Southern Counties

Edited by Sa

 Young**Writers**

First published in Great Britain in 2005 by:
Young Writers
Remus House
Coltsfoot Drive
Peterborough
PE2 9JX
Telephone: 01733 890066
Website: www.youngwriters.co.uk

SB ISBN 1 84602 225 8

Foreword

Young Writers was established in 1991 and has been passionately devoted to the promotion of reading and writing in children and young adults ever since. The quest continues today. Young Writers remains as committed to the fostering of burgeoning poetic and literary talent as ever.

This year's Young Writers competition has proven as vibrant and dynamic as ever and we are delighted to present a showcase of the best poetry from across the UK. Each poem has been carefully selected from a wealth of *Playground Poets* entries before ultimately being published in this, our thirteenth primary school poetry series.

Once again, we have been supremely impressed by the overall high quality of the entries we have received. The imagination, energy and creativity which has gone into each young writer's entry made choosing the best poems a challenging and often difficult but ultimately hugely rewarding task - the general high standard of the work submitted amply vindicating this opportunity to bring their poetry to a larger appreciative audience.

We sincerely hope you are pleased with our final selection and that you will enjoy *Playground Poets Southern Counties* for many years to come.

Contents

Jack Gibbs (9)	34
Robert Colton (8)	34
Richard Brown (9)	34
Joseph Bound (9)	34
Emily Pullen (8)	35
Christopher Pearn (9)	35
Callum Thorpe (9)	35
Isabelle Mills (9)	36
Ellie-May Chester (9)	36
Amy Brimmer (9)	36
Claudia Crisell (9)	37
Zoe Carter (9)	37
Stephanie Hatchett (9)	37
George Robson (9)	37
Timothy Chow (8)	38
Maria Green (8)	38
Connie Pletts (9)	39
Matthew Flood (9)	39
Janos Mouton (9)	39
Laura Evans (9)	40
Matthew Malt (9)	40
Benjamin Millman (9)	40
Amy Fountain (9)	41
Emily Jenkinson (8)	41
Thomas Li (9)	41
Sasha Cochrane (8)	42
Sophie Parsons (9)	42
Jordan Torrington (9)	42
Michael Wooldridge (9)	42
Christopher House (9)	43
Laura Starr (9)	43
Alex Hammond (9)	43
Shannon Fisk (9)	44
Tom Matthews (9)	44
Adam Marples (9)	44
Megan Sheppard (9)	45
Jack Banting (8)	45
Elizabeth Hatch (9)	45
Katie Blomley (8)	46
Steffan Thomas (8)	46
Alex McClarren (8)	46

Bordon Junior School, Bordon

Roseanna Cranmer (9)	47
Bradley Smith (10)	47
Drew Munn (11)	48
Daniel Snook (10)	48
Katrina Everett (10)	49
Amy Jaggers (10)	49
Kizzie Masters (10)	49
Shona Ryer (10)	50
Jordan Osborne (10)	50
Ryan Breakspear (11)	50
Vasemaca Ratukula (9)	51
Shannon Lindsay (9)	51
Elleanor Williams (10)	52
Joshua Scott (9)	52
Kimberley McDowall (9)	53
Jake Black (11)	54

Conifers Primary School, Weymouth

Tori Coltart (11)	54
Hannah Palmer (11)	55
Natalie Atkinson (11)	55
Chloe Bagwell (11)	55
Rebecca Bestwick (11)	56
Roxanne Cummins (11)	56
Carley Nash (11)	56
Joshua King (11)	57
Ian Ansell (11)	57
Daniel Bill (11)	58
George Cunningham (11)	58
Andrew McNulty (11)	58
Stefenee Grove (11)	59
Hazel Pritchard (11)	59
James Rosser (11)	59
Jack Hoskins (11)	60
Jasmine Lonsdale (11)	60
Joe Liggitt (11)	60
Sophie Hillier (11)	61
Christopher Edwards (11)	61
Aston Butcher (11)	61
Jade Marie Newman (11)	62

Hatch Warren Junior School, Basingstoke

Darren Minton (8)	62
Philip Christie (8)	63
Katie Mahoney (8)	64
Tom Mitchell (7)	65
Carla Russell (8)	65
Jessica Brady (8)	66
Arron Chapman (8)	66
Tayla Boote (8)	67
Leah Dorling (8)	67
Amy Knight (8)	68
Kayleigh Welton (8)	68

Kempshott Junior School, Basingstoke

Kerry-Anne Jacobs (11)	69
Harry Rudge (10)	69
Ryan Johnson (11)	70
Ryan Burn (11)	70
Kayleigh Moseley (11)	71
Danielle Tregent (10)	71
Emily Noakes (11)	72
Miles Pope (11)	72
Tom O'Hanlon (11)	73
Wayne Collins (11)	73
Emma Smith (11)	74
Christopher Hanson (11)	74
Alex May (11)	75
David Pullar (11)	75
Alex Morley (11)	76
Danielle Gill (10)	76
Phoebe Wright (11)	77
Hannah Willmott (11)	77
Ben Pescud (11)	78

Kinson Primary School, Bournemouth

Nathaniel Nelson & Luke Watson (11)	78
Amy Wareham (11)	79
Jasmine Gulliver & Cara Dee (10)	80
Natasha Fisher (11)	81
Sarah Onions (11) & Leanne Braddock (10)	82
Josh Cook & Jake Perkin (10)	82

Connor Threadingham (10) & Dominic Stott (9)   83

Langstone Junior School, Portsmouth
Samuel Crowe (11)   83
Lorna Street (10)   84
Bradley Sexton (10)   84
Katie Wyatt (11)   85
Craig Richardson (11)   85
Emily Day (11)   86
Amy Richards (11)   86
Jessica Hayward (11)   87
Paige Graham (11)   87
Laura Milwain (11)   87
Mae Ferrett (11)   88
Lucy Purcell (11)   88
Beth Scott (11)   89
Rebecca Stockley (10)   89
Georgia Chandler (11)   90
Bradley Allen (11)   90
Daniel Hardy (11)   91
Jack Woodroofe (10)   91
Tamzin Cormican (11)   92
Chay Pope (11)   92
Mark Leighton (11)   93
Joseph Smith (10)   93
Brooke Saunders (11)   94
Floss Pearce (10)   94
Zoe Martin (11)   95
Amber Haly (11)   95
Ashley Helm (10)   96
Samuel Wilkin (10)   96
Jamie Cooper (11)   97
Amy Turton (11)   97
Kate Willis (10)   98
Ellen Cooper (10)   99

Mill Rythe Junior School, Hayling Island
Yo Yo Hung (11)   99
Sasha Heathcote (11)   100
Jack Reynolds (10)   100
Chloe Kiellor (10)   100

Harry Hancock (11)	119
Connor Henry (10)	119
Nicola Emms (11)	119
Rachel Emms (11)	120
Sammy Price (11)	120
Katie Harland (11)	120
Bobby Coulter (11)	121
Emily Lewis (10)	121
Charlotte Hensby (11)	121
Jack Reed (11)	122
Annie Godwin (11)	122
Jessica Bone (11)	122
Matthew Bird (11)	123
Rachel Stanway (11)	123
Kimberley Mackey (11)	123

Rudgwick Primary School, Rudgwick

Harry Grace (8)	124
Sarah Twyford (8)	125
Kelsey Cairns (8)	125
Ryan Johnson (8)	126
Edward Webb (8)	126
Daniel Botting (8)	126
Rebecca Cornish (9)	127
Ryan Dunkley (7)	127
Amy Brown (8)	127
Sasha Newman (8)	128
Amy Sayers (8)	128
Nadia Dekany (8)	129
Emily Townsend (9)	129
Jessica Humphreys (8)	130
Rebecca Johnson (7)	130
Tiffany Allan (8)	131
Ian Etherington (7)	131

St Leonard's CE Primary School, St Leonards-on-sea

Elizabeth Meacher (11)	131
Megan Barnes (10)	132
Chloe Campbell (11)	132
Saffron Oliver (11)	133
Hollie Francis (11)	133

Ronnie Aubrey (11)	133
Mark Goodrum (10)	134
Bethany Ward (11)	134
Lily Loughman (11)	135
Merlin Webster (11)	135
Elliece Worboys (10)	136
Ryan Mills (11)	136
William Morrison (11)	137
Alice Moye (10)	137
Sean Robinson (11)	137
Daniel Price (11)	138
Hannah Withers (11)	138

St Margaret's Junior School, Midhurst

Annabel Hill (7)	139
Ellie Wood-Crainey (8)	139
Hamish Petty (8)	139
Lydia Marks (7)	140
Lydia Nethercott-Garabet (7)	140
Floss Pearce (7)	140
Mary Hunter (8)	141
Eliza Ingham (7)	141
Tom Condon (8)	141
Emily Gunter (7)	142
Holly Shellard (8)	142
Chloe Thomas (7)	142
Ben Pothecary (10)	143
Poppy Frazer (8)	143
Sarah Gill (11)	144
Laurence Bigos (11)	145
Travers Murgatroyd (10)	145
Catherine Beale (11)	146
Joanna Dearden (9)	146
George Foster (11)	147
Joe Shellard (11)	148
Charlotte Vergette (11)	149
Caitlin gape O'Donnell (10)	150
Izzie Hargreaves (10)	150
Harley Evans (11)	151
Emily Shaw (9)	152
Lottie MacCallum (10)	152

Skippers Hill Manor Preparatory School, Mayfield

The Poems

Snow

Snow, you're white
I see you at night
Your snowflakes are everywhere
You come for years, months or days
When you arrive to the year
I love you snow.

Karan Sharma (8)

The Playground Ghost

The playground ghost, she roams and rules
The Wendy house, the swings and pool.
She stole his socks, she took her shoes!
'I left them here, I wouldn't lose
them - Mummy said I mustn't!'
'Well Mummy's right, but you have not
obeyed her golden rule.'

The playground ghost, she has no name
And wears her uniform the same
As when she died from changing practice.
Her clothes they smell of sweat and tears
This is why she steals with fears
Children's belongings to lead them astray
As she was on that fateful day.

The children cry and teachers bored
Of hearing these ghost stories told
They haven't seen the playground ghost
But they imagine her like most
Children that forget and lose
And also scared of ghosts and ghouls
Will not meet the child of the past.

Plum Ayloff (10)
Ardingly College Junior School, Haywards Heath

My Imagination

I'm on the beach thinking about my thoughts,
Thinking about what it would be like to walk on water;
What it would be like to be a siren
To trick, to fool people into crashing!

The imagination of my mind is exploding in my head -
The sea lashing against the sand.
The blazing sun feels like it is eating me up;
I feel like I am in a wonderland.

The sound of the sea is like angels singing.
I feel like I am swimming with dolphins -
I am drifting away from reality.

Swimmers swimming, surfers surfing
And me alone on the beach,
So it seems in my mind.

Dulcie Irving (11)
Ardingly College Junior School, Haywards Heath

Coming First

The cool air blows on our faces
The shadows move as we run
The sound of our feet on the grass
Tired people begin to walk.

As you look behind you, you can't see anyone!
You feel scared and happy at the same time
You begin to slow down and don't know why.

You start to see everyone in front of you
As you get faster you trip and you can't run
You suddenly realise that lots of people are behind you and not in front

I get up and the finish line is in front of me
I sprint and I win, but I have hurt my leg!

Charlotte Olney (11)
Ardingly College Junior School, Haywards Heath

An Unusual Day

I was just walking
Silently on a normal day
When I saw animals all around me!

I saw lots of animals,
But doing everyday things,
I saw . . .

Monkeys wearing suits
And drinking tea!

Pandas throwing oranges everywhere,
Hitting other animals,
Split, splat, slap!

I walked past what I thought
Would be the school
I pass everyday,
But I saw a different building.

The unknown house let out
A high call,
Like a bird singing, ringing!

I looked up
Thinking I would see
A bird, but I saw a . . .

Flying dinosaur soaring
Swooping and
Squawking!

Passing me there were
Elephants rumbling, with smoke
Coming out of their tails!

I ran into my house
I sat down and
Thought and thought.

Emelie Fitzgerald (11)
Ardingly College Junior School, Haywards Heath

No, Michael!

(Inspired by Michael Rosen)

Good morning, Michael!
Yes, it's a wonderful day for a picnic
No, Michael - Ben is *not* the March Hare
And Harry is *not* the Mad Hatter
Even though the older children say they are!
They're just playing imaginary games -
And no, Michael - I am *not* the Queen of Hearts!
Now go back and play!

Back again, Michael?
Yes, I'm *sure* a pirate won't take you away
And builder's dog is not a panther.
Now I'll tell you once more -
The older children are just playing imaginary games!

Oh, Michael, what's wrong now?
You don't want to turn into an alien?
Well, I'm sure you won't!
No, I'm *not* a slimy, slippery alien!
Please, please, *please* try to understand
Children like to play imaginary games!

You're cold?
Well, you should've brought a coat in then
You're allergic to fish?
That's interesting . . .
No, the biscuits aren't really sardines
The science block is not an igloo.
Right, Michael, remember -
It's just imaginary games!

Excellent - that's the bell
And I won't be on duty again for a whole week!
No buts, Michael -
Just go back to class!

Kathryn Welsh (10)
Ardingly College Junior School, Haywards Heath

Humpty Dumpty's Tragic Accident!

(Inspired by Humpty Dumpty)

Humpty Dumpty fell off the wall
Humpty Dumpty had a great fall

All the king's men and all the king's soldiers
Couldn't repair the bump on his shoulders

Whilst Mrs Humpty hid in shame
Poor Mr Humpty howled with pain!

The Humpty children found it amusing
That on their dad's shoulders there was major bruising

In the hospital all bandaged up
Drinking green medicine out of a cup

Humpty Dumpty is lying there
Nibbling a rather unripe pear!

Now Humpty Dumpty is back on the wall
Thanking the Lord he survived his fall!

Joshua Williams (11)
Ardingly College Junior School, Haywards Heath

The Scorpion

Swiftly, smoothly it moves
Emerging from the sand
It's as fierce as a lion
Yet as quiet as a mouse
Its poisonous needle
Hanging right behind him!

He surely is the king!
He hides in small, dark places
Like shoes . . .
So . . . never leave your shoes outside
In the desert . . .
Or you might get a nasty sting!

Ross Gray (11)
Ardingly College Junior School, Haywards Heath

Am I Coming First Or Am I Coming Last?

Am I coming first or am I coming last?
The wind is whirling through my head . . .
And making me feel nervous.

The panting in my heart
Is thumping like a drum
I'm getting very tired
I hope it's nearly over.

I'm speeding like a cheetah
Trying to win the race
Will I win or will I lose?

I'm coming to the finish line
Where I hear the roaring crowds
I'm coming and it's soon to end
When I've passed the line . . . and I've won.

Chelsie Davidson (11)
Ardingly College Junior School, Haywards Heath

Sea Song

The soft, silent sea has a song to sing
Of pirates, pearls and distant shores;
But also of wind and wild, wild waves
Crashing and colliding with the shore,
As she sings her song of beauty.

Why does the sea ebb and flow?
Why does she show so many moods?
Why does she toss and turn so wildly
And yet lap so gently on the shore?

So often we fail to hear the sea's song
In our troubled world of clatter and noise.
But she's there, always there -
Immortal, immense, alive,
Singing her song of beauty . . .

Olivia Homewood (10)
Ardingly College Junior School, Haywards Heath

The Beach

Walking along the beach, my brother and me
Watching the waves crash on the shore . . .
Then dribbling back to the sea.

The sun shining brightly in our eyes
Virtually blinding us both
We look up - the seagulls are cackling
As though they were laughing
At something we had done.

The house is ahead in the distance
With Mum's arms waving high in the air
We greet her and smile.

Looking back at the distance we have covered
The footprints in the golden sand
That glistens in daylight.

We turn around,
Listening to the calm hush of the sea
Glad to be home, glad to see Mum.

Jack Harrison (11)
Ardingly College Junior School, Haywards Heath

The Animals And The Humans

Butterflies among the grass
The wonderful silence and peace
Flowers in their flowerbeds
Carpets of red and blue
A dragonfly skims across the murky pond
The silence is broken
A loud moaning and grunting noise
Echoes through the sky
The sun reflects off the monster's back
The tractor's wheels tear up the ground
The peace has gone from this beautiful place
Men have taken over . . .

Emily Baker (11)
Ardingly College Junior School, Haywards Heath

In My House . . .

In my house on the second floor,
Lives a horrible hairy monster.

He is tiny and as thin as a paper clip,
With a grumpy attitude.

Each time I see him,
I get a bizarre feeling
Being tiny and as thin as a paper clip just like him!

He has purple hair,
With a green body
And all his clothes are orange!

My hair is blonde,
With a white body
And my clothes are all different colours!

I do not see how
My mum is not scared of him
But then again she's always shouting at him

Sometimes I feel related,
Especially now I know . . .

The monster is . . .
. . . my big brother!

Elizabeth Gregory (11)
Ardingly College Junior School, Haywards Heath

The Playground Monster

The playground monster is big and hairy
And he is *very* scary!
With green and pink fur, a long, red tail
Big blue hands and bright-red feet.

The playground monster's biggest treat is . . .
No, not a cake or coke
That stuff only makes him choke!
His favourite treat is a discarded blazer
An old tennis ball
Or something that belongs to you or me!

When he sees that lovely treat
He drools and licks his lips
He creeps and crawls towards his goal and then . . .
Gobble! Crunch!
Gulp! Munch!

Then the cries start,
'Where's my blazer?'
'Where's my ball?'
'Oh no, my pencil case!'

You know the monster's been
When a child loses one of their things
I wonder why he only comes when a child misplaces
One of their things?

Amelia Riis (11)
Ardingly College Junior School, Haywards Heath

The Boy

(Inspired by Little Miss Muffet)

There was once a boy
All on his own
Feeling so sorry for himself . . .
Then along came a girl
Who sat beside him
And helped the poor boy
To feel better.

They gradually became good friends
And they laughed and played together
They had so much fun that day
And when it was time to go to class
They hurried in together.

Glad, so glad to be such good friends!

Matthew Rawbin (11)
Ardingly College Junior School, Haywards Heath

Race, Race

Bang! The race has started and we're off!
I feel as nervous as can be
I hear people all around me, gasping for air
The wind is whistling in my face
I look around, I am first . . . at the moment . . .
Can I keep going?
Yes! I've overtaken loads of people
Breathe in, breathe deeply . . .
Oh no!
A rotting root reaches for my foot!
Grabs it, twists it - the pain! The pain!
But I must run on and on and on . . .
Yippee! I can see the finish - I must speed up
There's the funnel - run, run, run . . .
I've done it, I really have!

Amy Groome (10)
Ardingly College Junior School, Haywards Heath

A Teacher's Duty

(Inspired by Michael Rosen)

Bradley Bniffuls, why on earth did you push that boy over
And make him cry?
Don't cry - just tell me -
I can't understand what you are saying!

Frederick, stop crying and go to matron, *please!*
Bradley - come back here now!
I haven't finished talking to you!
Bradley - come back by the count of three -
One, two, *Bradley!*
Go to the headmaster
And explain what you've done!

Yes, Zoe, what is it?
Yes, Zoe, we are going on a trip on Friday
No Zoe, don't bring your dog, cat or hamster
No, Zoe, don't bring your mother
She'll be fine at home!

Is what Lucy said true?
Did you put a big, black banana in your fist
And then squash it in her face, Tim?
Well, did you?
I don't really want to know -
Go and clean yourself up, Lucy.
Tim - go to the headmaster -
I'm going to the staffroom
I can't take anymore!

Anna Cook (11)
Ardingly College Junior School, Haywards Heath

The Drummer

Playing on my drums
Causing a huge commotion
Mum shouting;
'All I can hear is *bang, bang, bang*
and a *crash* and a *splash*
as you play your drums!'

My mother then cries:
'Ow! Ow! My head hurts!
My ears hurt! Please -
Play something soothing,
My son, you're shattering
The peace right now!
And all I can hear is *bang, bang, bang*
And a *crash* and a *splash*
As you play your drums!'

'Son, stop that playing,
you're going to bring the
house down with an explosion
like you've got dynamite
And all I can hear is
Bang, bang, bang and a
Crash and a *splash*
As you play your drums!'

'Son! Son! You've brought the house down
now there is nowhere to live
So stop that playing.'
But all I do is keep on banging!

James Hepher (11)
Ardingly College Junior School, Haywards Heath

Sally, Sally, Sally

Once there was a girl called Sally
Sally was unpopular
She had no friends.
One day while walking in the playground
She came across a bottle,
She picked it up and thought,
I could make this a game!

Later that day, Bully Boy Bob
Ran into Sally.
Crash! She dropped her bottle.
'Oh, Bob, you're like a wrestler,' Sally said.
But strangely . . .
Red smoke was rising from the bottle!
Bully Boy Bob ran fast away,
Sally didn't.

A genie appeared,
'I will grant your every wish!'
Sally, in fear, ran to Mrs James.
'Mrs James, help!'
'What is it?'
'Just come!' Sally pleaded.

She approached the genie,
'Now just go away
Or I will unleash my detention power!'
'Go on then,' the genie jeered.
'OK . . .'
'Aaaaargh,'
And the genie was gone!

I don't know how
But that's how it happened,
And no Sally is no longer unpopular
Or left out . . .
So perhaps the magic did work after all?

Stanley Porthouse (11)
Ardingly College Junior School, Haywards Heath

Grass

Grass grows everywhere
God planted it too
Be very careful with it
Or it will get stuck to your shoe.

Grass grows with water
Sunlight and air
Watching it will take forever
So grab some tea and a chair.

You'll find grass in gardens
Forests and parks
Drawing grass is easy
They look like little sparks.

Grass is all over the world
It's a very common plant
If only relatives were common like that
Like an uncle or an aunt.

Alison Durham (9)
Berrywood Primary School, Southampton

Apples

Apples are nice
Apples are red
Apples are clean
Apples are green
Apples are sweet
And give you
A treat.

George Dufty (8)
Berrywood Primary School, Southampton

Stripy Cat

Stripy cat crawls
Along the walls
And goes in for food
At dinner time.

Then he catches mice
Which are very nice
But not for me
Nor you.

He plays all day
Then hides in the hay
And neither me, nor anyone
Can find him.

Then at night
When there's no light
He hunts
For smaller animals.

Benjamin Greenwood (9)
Berrywood Primary School, Southampton

The Crocodile

A river lover
A snappy creature
A fishy eater
A slow walker
A spiky predator
A silent stalker
A deer attacker.

Hannah Goldsmith (9)
Berrywood Primary School, Southampton

A Loving Tiger

A prowling roarer
A gentle walker
A meat eater
A scary scratcher
A fine swimmer
A sharp biter
A low hider
A high jumper

An amazing player
A quick runner
A long sleeper
A turning turner
A family lover
A furry fluffer
A stripy stranger
A jungle liver
A loving tiger!

Lauren Parsons (9)
Berrywood Primary School, Southampton

Green Trees

The tree   can
Hear   humming
Birds   high up
In the trees
The tree is as green
As lime
The tree can see for miles and miles.
The canopy is so blowy that
You might get blown away
The tree has a chill
When there is a snake climbing
Up a branch.

Hannah Symes (8)
Berrywood Primary School, Southampton

Mr Cat

They're furry
They're cuddly
Their paws are smooth.

They hunt for food
Their claws are sharp
Their ears are pricked
They say, 'Miaow'.

They have kittens

They're *cats!*

George Carter (9)
Berrywood Primary School, Southampton

There Once Was A Girl Called Carole

There once was a girl called Carole
Who lived in a brown, wooden barrel,
One rainy day
It rolled away
And that was the end of poor Carole.

Rebecca Simmons (9)
Berrywood Primary School, Southampton

Tiger

A stripy hunter
A hungry eater
A scary creature
A fast runner
A good smeller.

Todd Ackerman (8)
Berrywood Primary School, Southampton

The Cat

A magnificent jumper
A lazy creature
A fast eater
A fly catcher
A toy squeaker
A stripy sleeper
A fast pouncer
A set of teeth that get sharper and sharper.

Zak Brightman (9)
Berrywood Primary School, Southampton

The Rainforest Tree

The tree is as big as the sky
It can see into the blue heaven
The wind tickles the tree
The tree can feel the wind rush past
It can hear the song of the really noisy animals.

Ben Hayes (8)
Berrywood Primary School, Southampton

Guy

There once was a chap called Guy
Who was tall, but extremely sly
He jumped in a boat
Which could not stay afloat
And that was the end of sly Guy.

Gabe Petty (8)
Berrywood Primary School, Southampton

Anaconda

A ground seeker
A skin shedder
A crocodile eater
An egg stealer
A spider killer
A fast eater
A ground slitherer
A tree climber
A rat killer
An animal fisher.

Lewis Cozens (8)
Berrywood Primary School, Southampton

What A Tree Can See

A tree is bright, lush and is as tall as a hotel
I can see lots of people working in partners on passages
I can feel insects crawling all over me.

I can hear the birds singing and insects munching
And people singing their one
Song with their little tune.

Aleisha Mouton (7)
Berrywood Primary School, Southampton

Butterfly

Butterflies see leaves swooping to the ground
The sound that it can hear is a storm coming
And a tiger roaring
It feels scary flying on the canopy
Whirling above the clouds
And eating on the flowers.

Holly Cooper (8)
Berrywood Primary School, Southampton

Rainforests

Down in the jungle, the
        Dark green jungle,
A monkey and a big cat play
The large giant leaves act
        As a canopy,
Keeping them all dry, all day.

There's lots of life in the rainforests
From tiny insects to snakes,
There's beauty and death,
        All that is life
We fear that this jungle may break.

Lucy Armstrong (8)
Berrywood Primary School, Southampton

Trees, Trees

Trees, trees rustle in the breeze
Tall as me and as tall as a beast
Trees, trees wonderful as a crane
Squawking in the breeze.

Jack Bailey (8)
Berrywood Primary School, Southampton

Trees, Trees

Trees, trees, beautiful trees
You are blowing in the breeze
And I can feel the freeze!
You are as tall as a skyscraper
So I will put you in the paper!

Dominic Harrison (7)
Berrywood Primary School, Southampton

Animal World

I can hear a sound
Like this ooh, ooh ahah
Ooh, ooh, ah, ah, oie, oie
They're so noisy
I'm going to faint, the loggers are noisy too
Chop, chop, chop
The tigers are scaring me
Roar, roar, roar
I can hear the grasshoppers squeaking.

Harry Mulcahy (8)
Berrywood Primary School, Southampton

The Beautiful Rainforest

Trees are lush
Trees are beautiful
They spread out like an umbrella
The trees see me
I see the tree
I am being tickled by animals
I can hear the tiger coming.

Eleanor Denny (8)
Berrywood Primary School, Southampton

Summer

She is a bowl of fruit arrangement
She hears through blueberry ears
She talks through rosemary lips
Her cheeks are as bright as a peach
And her eyes gleam in the night.

Charlotte Mackey (8)
Berrywood Primary School, Southampton

The Rainforest

I can see a tall, fat tree with branches coming off
On the branches there are light green, lush leaves
With a chocolate brown trunk
The tree can see a tiger and a monkey swinging through the trees
And a bright green snake wrapped around the branches
The beautiful tree can feel the monkey holding on tightly to its
branches
And there is a snake around the tree
The tree can hear the river hitting the grey rocks by the bank.

Kate Redfern (8)
Berrywood Primary School, Southampton

The Life Of The Rainforest

I can feel the wildlife
Crawling over me,
Oooo, ah, ah
My leaves are as green as apples
And I can hear many birds flying over me
I can see a tiger coming, looking for its prey
It yawns, I can see its terrible jaws
When it roars, it scares the wildlife away.

Lewis Hutchinson (7)
Berrywood Primary School, Southampton

What Can Trees Do?

It is a big tree
It can see
It can see animals as small as a pea
It can feel
It can feel a tiny flea.

Molly Dowse (8)
Berrywood Primary School, Southampton

Rainforest Butterfly

Fly, fly, make your dream, soar above like a rainforest beam!
You're so cool and colourful so you deserve to live
You were once a caterpillar and a cocoon.
You wanted to be you and now your wish is true!
You don't want four wings
You want more!
But it's the way you were born so stick with it!
You'll only live for two or three days
What a shame is that?
But those days are now gone, so goodbye butterfly!

Louise Price (8)
Berrywood Primary School, Southampton

Rainforest

Beetles chattering
Trees rattling
The bees are buzzing
In the air
The wind is blowing
My hair is flowing
Creatures jumping everywhere.

Jamie Abbott (8)
Berrywood Primary School, Southampton

The Rainforest Poem

The wind is blowing my branches
I can hear birds and toucans
The monkey is jumping on my branches
I can see a lion growling.

Brad Gilbert (7)
Berrywood Primary School, Southampton

Parrots And Birds

Parrots flying through the forest
Then there's the birds just flying for fun
I know it's silly, but that's the game.
Come and have fun flying and playing a game in the air
Come and have a go it's jolly good fun for everyone
Don't you think?
It's just for fun.

Hester Lewis (8)
Berrywood Primary School, Southampton

Rainforest

I see . . .
Scratching monkeys all over in the trees
Even taller than you and me
I feel thirsty because of all the heat and steam
Rainforest bright and beautiful in the sunshine
All day long frogs are leaping joyfully in the rainforest on the floor.

Helen Price (8)
Berrywood Primary School, Southampton

Jaguars

In the jungle
Where the temperature is hot
The jaguars come out
They sneak through the jungle
As the weather gets hotter
Watch out!

Jack Duddridge (8)
Berrywood Primary School, Southampton

Trees I See

In a tree I see
A scorpion sting everything he sees
I see a monkey meeting every other monkey in the tree.

I see trees
Beautiful trees
I see, I see, I see
Trees.

Samantha Hastie (8)
Berrywood Primary School, Southampton

Rainforest

Tall trees, dripping rain
Scorpions scratching, evil eagles
Slow sloths, leaping monkeys
Snapping crocodiles, fast cheetahs
Insects itching underground.

Richie Brimmer (7)
Berrywood Primary School, Southampton

Rainforest Life

Snipping scorpions, snip, snip, snip
Burning bites on my skin
Squealing monkeys oh, ah, ah
Sweat goes down my hot spine
Hot, hot, hot.

Isabella Mabey (7)
Berrywood Primary School, Southampton

The Rainforest

R ainfall dripping
A snake slithering
I nsects creeping
N ight bats flying
F orest animals moving
O utside leaves waving
R eaching monkeys
E xciting elephants
S piders biting
T rees cut down.

Bijia Wu (7)
Berrywood Primary School, Southampton

The Amazing Rainforest

Rainforest, rainforest
The birds and bees
Are on the trees
The breeze has gone
Past the trees with
The bees.

Alexander Hallett (7)
Berrywood Primary School, Southampton

Rainforest

Scorpion stings
Many things
Frogs leap
Jaguar sleep
Beetles rattling
Everyone tattling.

Miles Rogers (8)
Berrywood Primary School, Southampton

Rainforest

R ainforest, so many colours, monkeys swinging from branch to
branch
A nimals, there are so many, fish gliding under the blue, clear water
I t is such a peaceful place with birds singing in the trees
N ever crouch down in a rainforest you never know if a tiger is going
to pounce on you.
F orest, you can't call it a forest, this is paradise
O h no, what have we here? No we can't do this, cutting down trees,
no we can't
R ainforest are now disappearing quickly
E ast not east, they are doing it as well, can we stop this?
S end all the armies, we must stop this
T arantulas and tigers – save them, we have to stop this *now!*

Amy Darling (8)
Berrywood Primary School, Southampton

Save The Rainforest

Trees as green as a frog
Monkeys swing from the canopy, side to side they go
Thunder crashes, it goes deep, deep in the heart of the rainforest.
Here comes the tree cutter.
Can we save the rainforest?
Go! Go! Go!

Claudia Speed (8)
Berrywood Primary School, Southampton

Parrot

The bright, beautiful parrot spreads out his colourful, blue, fluffy wings
The bright boiling sun shines on the beautiful, colourful bird
He swoops round the muddy rainforest listening
To animals around the large rustling forest.

Alexander Allen (8)
Berrywood Primary School, Southampton

Save The Trees

The rainforest is dying.
All you can hear are the sounds of the falling trees,
The loggers never stop
The monkeys can't swing from tree to tree
The birds can't fly because air is polluted
The fish's water is full of dark smoke
The animals' homes are disappearing and species are being wiped out
So help me save the rainforest
Do it for the frogs, snakes, parrots and the big cats
The oxygen is going and we need it to live
The sounds of rustling trees is going
The loggers can't hear you when you say, 'stop cutting down trees'.
Their heavy chainsaws are all you can hear.
So help me save the rainforest.

Joe Evans (7)
Berrywood Primary School, Southampton

Deforestation

D estroyers are cutting down trees
E verything is dying
F orest animals are worrying
O ranges are falling down
R ivers get longer
E veryone is escaping
S alamanders are creeping
T oucans are flying
A nimals are going
T igers are searching
I nside the forest it's like a hurricane
O n the forest floor there are lots of tree trunks
N othing is coming back.

Samuel Dell (8)
Berrywood Primary School, Southampton

Rainforests Are Colourful

Rainforests are really colourful
With swinging monkeys
Thunder striking down on the floor
Tarantulas crawling over a lizard
People coming out of the door
A blue sky and a hot sunny day
Snakes slithering along the ground.

Jamie Butters (8)
Berrywood Primary School, Southampton

Amazon Rainforest

Deep in the heart of the Amazon rainforest
You can sometimes hear chirping from grasshoppers
And squawking from monkeys

But there is less and less of this every day because
We are cutting down trees.
               Stop!

George Culley (8)
Berrywood Primary School, Southampton

Rainforest

As the monkeys swing from tree to tree
Parrots squawk like screaming children
Leaves rustle when the wind blows
It frightens little animals
Here comes the wood cutter
A shame another tree went.

George Lockyer (8)
Berrywood Primary School, Southampton

Rainforests

R ocky paths are all through the rainforest
A nimals lay upon their home
I n fact they can only see us
N ever see a bug crawling up you
F rogs jump all around you and poisonous ones
O ranges fall from up above and hit you on the head
R ainforest is in danger, can you help it?
E ast Amazon is a dangerous place
S mall animals climb from tree to tree
T hunder crashing through the huge rainforest.

Alice Glendinning (8)
Berrywood Primary School, Southampton

Rainforests Are Green

Rainforests are green, fit to be seen
Tree frogs jumping from branch to branch
Rainforest trees are good to block the breeze
Thunder crashes like a *bang!*

Jacob Pembroke-Burn (8)
Berrywood Primary School, Southampton

Rainforest Environment

Monkeys swing and the bushes sway
The light green canopy up in the sky
While the vines sway away
And the rivers pass by
Tigers prowling as birds fly away.

Alice Stubbington (8)
Berrywood Primary School, Southampton

Animal Sounds

Tarantulas scuttling
In the rainforest
Toucans and parrots
Squawking, I can hear them
Birds chirping all around
Tigers roaring, uh oh!
Run away!

Olivia Jennings (8)
Berrywood Primary School, Southampton

Animals From The Rainforest

Monkeys swing from vines
Dangling from the bushy green canopy
While the river Amazon rushes past
Monkey-eating eagles spy on their prey
Suddenly they swoop down and *kill!*

Rachel Matthews (8)
Berrywood Primary School, Southampton

Animals In The Rainforest

Monkeys swing from branch to branch eating as they go
But beware of a tarantula stepping on your toe
You might see a frog jumping up and down
And birds singing gracefully, making a lovely sound.

Abbie Willis (8)
Berrywood Primary School, Southampton

Ecuadorian Rainforest Poetry

Trees are as green as the grass
Lakes are as blue as the sky
Nature glides through the forest
Deep in the heart of the Ecuadorian rainforest

Monkeys call across the east
The eagle flies to catch his prey
Nature glides through the forest
Deep in the heart of the Ecuadorian rainforest.

Daniel Lowe (8)
Berrywood Primary School, Southampton

My Pet Tortoise

A slow walker
A non-talker
A cucumber lover
A grass stomper
A shell crasher
A quiet critter
A beautiful feller
A great lawnmower.

Karina Diaz (9)
Berrywood Primary School, Southampton

It's Green, It's Brown

It's green, it's brown, the sky is bright blue
It's yellow and orange like an orange teddy bear
It's green, it's brown, the sky is dark blue
The trees are swaying, the monkeys swing from tree to tree
The frogs are jumping all over the land
And the parrots squawking like children.

Lucy Robertson (8)
Berrywood Primary School, Southampton

My Friend Chris

A Game Cube master
A sports player
A pizza hater
A fast food lover
A quick runner
A TV watcher
A fantastic dancer
A Portsmouth supporter.

Jack Turner (9)
Berrywood Primary School, Southampton

Sporty Joe

A super swimmer
A speedy runner
A very fast cycler
A karate chopper
A meat eater
A sumo slammer
A head beater.

Adam Finnerty (8)
Berrywood Primary School, Southampton

Me!

A hair geller
A TV watcher
A PlayStation master
A Chelsea and Saints lover
A fast eater
A fast rider
A good striker
A skateboarding lover.

Daniel Lyon (8)
Berrywood Primary School, Southampton

Me

A non-stop talker
A football player
A PlayStation master
A Pompey lover.

Jack Gibbs (9)
Berrywood Primary School, Southampton

Rainforest Tree

T rees as tall as the sky
R ain pours over the forest
E quador has wonderful things that fly
E asy steps and you'll survive.

Robert Colton (8)
Berrywood Primary School, Southampton

My Dogs Are Cute

My dogs are brown as chocolate
They always bark at strangers
They eat meat and biscuits
And love to walk.

Richard Brown (9)
Berrywood Primary School, Southampton

Me

A fast eater
A super player
A PlayStation master
A Saints supporter.

Joseph Bound (9)
Berrywood Primary School, Southampton

A Super Dolphin

A super swimmer
A fab jumper
A colourful flipper
A deep-blue colour
A fish lover
A turning diver
A super turner
A lovely singer
An amazing sea creature!

Emily Pullen (8)
Berrywood Primary School, Southampton

What Am I?

A good hopper
A carrot chomper
A quiet stomper
An attentive listener
A floppy ear bumper
A great stopper.

Christopher Pearn (9)
Berrywood Primary School, Southampton

Slither

Slither,
        Slither,
                Slither,
All across the ground
Do you need legs when all you need to do
Is slither, slither, slither.

Callum Thorpe (9)
Berrywood Primary School, Southampton

Horse In The Mist

Horse in the mist
Appear very faintly
He neighs in the wind
He walks through the cold
He canters to the moon
He gallops across the sunset
He drinks from the watering hole
He gazes in the breeze
He feeds off the luscious grass
He neighs in the night
The horse in the mist.

Isabelle Mills (9)
Berrywood Primary School, Southampton

My Dog

My dog has a furry coat,
Soft and brown
I like to take him for a walk
He loves the pond and getting dirty
I love his wet, black nose.

Ellie-May Chester (9)
Berrywood Primary School, Southampton

The Small Mouse

The mouse was small
With a very long tail and soft cuddly white fur
Squeak, squeak, have you noticed my long tail?
I am a mouse in a lovely warm house
I eat cheese, it is my favourite food.

Amy Brimmer (9)
Berrywood Primary School, Southampton

The Robber

A bad stealer
A noisy feeler
A clumsy leader
A continuous eater.

Claudia Crisell (9)
Berrywood Primary School, Southampton

A Bird

A nest maker
A worm stealer
An egg hatcher
A chick mother.

Zoe Carter (9)
Berrywood Primary School, Southampton

Zoe

A fast runner
A determined player
A Saints supporter
A friend maker
A great smiler.

Stephanie Hatchett (9)
Berrywood Primary School, Southampton

Snake!

Slither, slither, slither going across the ground
Faster and faster and poison in its fangs
Aah!

George Robson (9)
Berrywood Primary School, Southampton

Sportsman

A rugby player
A football fouler
A sumo slammer
A horsy rider

A slowcoach racer
A disastrous hurdler
A mischievous hammer thrower
A record breaker

A cunning coacher
A funky dancer
A silly ballerina
A karate chopper

A strengthening stamina
A crazy cricketer
A wonky weightlifter
A big winner!

Timothy Chow (8)
Berrywood Primary School, Southampton

The Lion

A meat eater
A blood drinker
A roar maker
An animal hunter
A skin ripper
A heart shaker
A human hugger.

Maria Green (8)
Berrywood Primary School, Southampton

My Dog

His big, fat face
His small, pea-sized eyes
His wet, rough tongue
With spots from his lies.

His plump, round body
His big, bushy tail
His slow, slow walk
When he fetches the mail.

His small, thin whiskers
His plodding, front paws
He growls when you push him
But he doesn't show his claws.

Connie Pletts (9)
Berrywood Primary School, Southampton

The Woman In 1,000,000 Plasters

There was a woman of Lasters
Who had 1,000,000 plasters
She saw a job
To get rid of a cat
And then she knew that she was a master.

Matthew Flood (9)
Berrywood Primary School, Southampton

Myself

A PlayStation freak
A Southampton supporter
A football lover
A Pompey hater!

Janos Mouton (9)
Berrywood Primary School, Southampton

Drinks

Drinks come in bottles
Drinks come in cans
Drinks come in little cups
So give them to your nans!
Drinks come in fountains
Drink and drink the lot
Don't drink them in your brother's room
'Cause you'll find you wet the cot
Drinks can be orange juice
They can be blackcurrant
They can even be appleade
That makes you burp a lot.

Laura Evans (9)
Berrywood Primary School, Southampton

My Brother

A fantastic talker
A PlayStation player
A Big Sats hater
A TV watcher
And a Simpson's lover.

Matthew Malt (9)
Berrywood Primary School, Southampton

Sam

Sam, Sam loved his jam
Especially on brown toast.
He thought it was nice
Before he met Baby Spice
But now he liked her most.

Benjamin Millman (9)
Berrywood Primary School, Southampton

Me

A horse lover
A terrible skater
A cool rocker
A brilliant guitar player
An Arsenal lover
A lovely daughter
A dog walker.

Amy Fountain (9)
Berrywood Primary School, Southampton

Me

A football player
A fantastic runner
A good swimmer
A Saints lover
A strawberry eater
A sporty daughter.

Emily Jenkinson (8)
Berrywood Primary School, Southampton

Untitled

There once was a boy called Tom
Who lit a nuclear bomb
He didn't stand back
And ate a Big Mac
And couldn't run away from the bomb.

Thomas Li (9)
Berrywood Primary School, Southampton

Hamster

A lazy sleeper
A food stacker
A fast digger
A brilliant climber.

Sasha Cochrane (8)
Berrywood Primary School, Southampton

Doggies

A loud barker
A fierce fighter
A fluffy lover
A settee hogger.

Sophie Parsons (9)
Berrywood Primary School, Southampton

Tiger

A food stalker
A claw poker
A fang fighter
A continuous growler.

Jordan Torrington (9)
Berrywood Primary School, Southampton

Cheetah

A fast runner
An antelope eater
A spotty tiger
A pouncing master.

Michael Wooldridge (9)
Berrywood Primary School, Southampton

Pirates

Pirates puke over stormy trees
Something green comes rolling along; peas!
An old man came so small
He was nothing at all
Pirates trip up and get bruised knees.

Christopher House (9)
Berrywood Primary School, Southampton

All About Me

An animal lover
A chocolate eater
A pea hater
A great reader
A good horse rider
A coke drinker.

Laura Starr (9)
Berrywood Primary School, Southampton

Snail

A snail is the slowest creature ever
It has got a very hard shell
Its head is like a squishy thing
It has eyes smaller than a pea that has not grown
It has a mouth like a newborn clam.

Alex Hammond (9)
Berrywood Primary School, Southampton

Lunchtime

Lunchtime where we play
Lunchtime where we pray
Lunchtime where we like to talk
Lunchtime where we walk
Lunchtime where the teachers watch
Lunchtime where we hopscotch.

Lunchtime's fun
Lunchtime's great
Lunchtime the best time at school.

Lunchtime where the toys come out
Lunchtime where people shout
Lunchtime where the fun begins
Lunchtime when we get our food out of tins
Lunchtime when everyone joins in.

Shannon Fisk (9)
Berrywood Primary School, Southampton

Me

A food lover
A PlayStation player
A football liker
A cat lover
A Stephanie lover.

Tom Matthews (9)
Berrywood Primary School, Southampton

Tigers

A dangerous predator
A roar maker
A meat eater
A stripy cheetah.

Adam Marples (9)
Berrywood Primary School, Southampton

My Cat

A purring creature
A biscuit eater
A scratching stranger
A milk lapper
A food smeller
A fish nipper.

Megan Sheppard (9)
Berrywood Primary School, Southampton

Dog

A bone licker
A stick fetcher
A ball catcher
A loud barker
A cat hater.

Jack Banting (8)
Berrywood Primary School, Southampton

Cat

A fast runner
A brilliant climber
A sneaky hunter
A good scratcher.

Elizabeth Hatch (9)
Berrywood Primary School, Southampton

The Fat Cat Is Back

There once was a big fluffy cat
Who liked to wear silly hats
He was so small
He got lost in the hall
When he sat on the bright yellow mat.

Katie Blomley (8)
Berrywood Primary School, Southampton

Bob

There once was a boy called Bob
Who was a bit of a slob
He went for a walk
To buy some pork
And came back as a bit of a snob.

Steffan Thomas (8)
Berrywood Primary School, Southampton

Stan

There once was a man called Stan
Who had a brain like a can
He ran up the lane
In the pouring rain
And went for a ride on a tram.

Alex McClarren (8)
Berrywood Primary School, Southampton

The Eye Of The Storm

In the mist of the mountains a storm blew up
Suddenly everything went quiet
Everything went icy cold
A sharp shiver ran down my spine
The sun stopped shining
The rivers stopped flowing
Everything was silent
Then the wind started howling like a wolf
A dark shadow suddenly fell over me
The earth started rumbling
Rain pelting down
Stabbing me like icicles
Piercing my skin
Trees flying everywhere
Cars and lorries spinning around like little leaves.

Roseanna Cranmer (9)
Bordon Junior School, Bordon

Floating Through Space

Floating through space, just watching the colourful planets drift by
No matter how close you think you are –
Could you reach out and touch a star?
They're just too far away
The stars look like golden tiny dots!
What's that? It's so big and colourful!
Look! Look! At those rings of flying rocks
As you drift further away they metamorphose
Into tiny specks of dust . . .

Bradley Smith (10)
Bordon Junior School, Bordon

The Beach

Salty spray whipping from the ocean,
Stinging our faces whenever we look out to sea,
Waves towering above us,
Roaring to their foamy end,
Wind high above our heads,
Hurling seagulls to their doom,
Accelerating clouds smother the sky
Beating us with merciless rain,
Sea engulfing the sands, then
Retreating to its watery lair
Explosions of frothing water
Throwing seaweed at us in vain
'Be calm,' says the sun
Emerging again
At last there is peace.

Drew Munn (11)
Bordon Junior School, Bordon

Gran, Can You Rap?

(Inspired by 'Gran, Can You Rap?' by Jack Ousbey)

She rapped down the motorway
She rapped in the hall
She rapped on the aeroplane
She rapped on the floor.

She's the best in the west
She's going to beat all the rest
She's the best rapping queen I've ever seen.

She rapped in the past
She rapped in the bath
She rapped in the future
And on to the path.

Daniel Snook (10)
Bordon Junior School, Bordon

Earth And Beyond

Here I am stuck in space
Astronauts are whizzing around me
The steaming sun is gleaming at me
It feels like Mars is a massive fireball coming towards me
Venus is glowing up like a torch
As I struggle upward gravity is pulling me down, down, down . . .
Mercury is as blue as the sky with clouds bulging round it
Now that it is night
The stars are lighting up
The moon is turning bright like a lantern in a black sea.

Katrina Everett (10)
Bordon Junior School, Bordon

The Space Rap

I rapped around the sun
And burnt my bum and it started
To sizzle like chips.

I rapped past Mars and saw a space car
And it looked like the famous North Star.

I'm a chip-clip, ship-flip, gripping space-shipping
Hip-hop queen.

Amy Jaggers (10)
Bordon Junior School, Bordon

Studland Beach

The tormenting waves consuming the beach
The needle-like rain plunging in to my face
The traumatising wind fighting mysteriously with the trees
The sky transforming into a black death hole
The ground becoming a muddy swamp.

Kizzie Masters (10)
Bordon Junior School, Bordon

Reflections

As the rain fell down I stood, meaningless.
The wind howling as never before.
Never in my life had I felt so cold.
I felt dead; my lips were blue.
The sea crashed and banged before our eyes
Then dwindled away.
The dark weather, cloudy and bored as a sulky child.
The air marbling as the frost crumbled.
The sharp, sharp touch of the wind on my face.

Shona Ryer (10)
Bordon Junior School, Bordon

Gran, Can You Rap?

(Inspired by 'Gran, Can You Rap?' by Jack Ousbey)

She rapped in the tunnel and got on the train
And rapped past the driver and rapped in the main
She said to me, 'I'm the mean, lean. Tip-top, hip-hop, rip-rap queen,'
She rapped in the future and rapped in the past
Who said rap wasn't fit to last?
She rapped past Buddy Holly and good golly Miss Molly
And she jammed and said, 'I'm way ahead coz
I'm a tip-top, hip-hop, rip-rap queen.'

Jordan Osborne (10)
Bordon Junior School, Bordon

Studland Beach

The waves and beach having a battle
The rain trying to murder the land
Bucking horses leading the attack
Deserted seaweed, purple with anger
Paths strewn dark green with
Corpses.

Ryan Breakspear (11)
Bordon Junior School, Bordon

Gran, Can You Rap?
(Inspired by 'Gran, Can You Rap?' by Jack Ousbey)

She rapped in the future
She rapped in the past
She rapped past the pool
She rapped past my school
Oh she's the best rapping gran, the world's ever seen
Oh now I believe she's the best rapping queen.
I'm a . . .
Tip-top, slip-slap
Hip-hop, trip-trap
Nip-nap, yip-yap
Happy, happy
Rap, rap
Queen.

Vasemaca Ratukula (9)
Bordon Junior School, Bordon

The Solar System

Here I am stranded in space, pitch-black, I can't see a thing
Wait a minute, everything is coming to life,
Tiny spots of glittering stars and far away planets galloping towards
me,
I see Mercury, tiny craters scattered around the dazzling planet,
It looks like a bird's egg spinning on its axis waiting to hatch,
Here's the next planet, it's Venus
This planet boiling away with excitement letting off its aroma whenever
it pleases
Finally back to planet Earth with the blue shining seas and green,
green grass.

Now I am back where I belong.

Shannon Lindsay (9)
Bordon Junior School, Bordon

Gran, Can You Rap?

(Inspired by 'Gran, Can You Rap?' by Jack Ousbey)

She rapped in her chair and spun around the floor
She rapped through the hall and went out the door
I'm the best rapping gran this world's ever seen
I'm a tip-top, slip-slap, rap-rap queen.

I rapped in the bath and through the door
I rapped in the 1939 war
I am the best rapping gran this world's ever seen
I'm a nip-nap, yip-yap, rap-rap queen.

I rapped through the hall
And turned really tall
And then went back really small
I'm the best rapping gran this world's ever seen
I'm a drip-drap, tip-tap, rap-rap queen.

Elleanor Williams (10)
Bordon Junior School, Bordon

My Rap: Space Planets

He rapped through Venus
Do you think the alien's seen us?
He rapped around Mars
Eating chocolate bars
He's the best rapping spaceman the galaxy's ever seen
He's a rip-rap, clip-clap, moon-goon, taz-baz, rip-rap king.

He rapped round Saturn drawing a pattern
He rapped around the sun
He burnt his bum.
He's the best rapping spaceman the galaxy's ever seen
He's a rip-rap, slip-slap, clip-clap, moon-goon, taz-baz, rip-rap king.

Joshua Scott (9)
Bordon Junior School, Bordon

I'm A Gymnastic

I swing on the bars
Past the moon and the stars

I'm a gymnastic
I feel fantastic

I balance on the beam
Being famous I dream

I'm a gymnastic
I feel fantastic

I dance on the floor
They cheer for more

I'm a gymnastic
I feel fantastic

I jump from the vault
And do a somersault

I'm a gymnastic
I feel fantastic

My total score
Was nine point four

I'm a gymnastic
I feel fantastic

Wearing my medal I feel proud
And this is what I shout out loud,

'I'm a gymnastic
I feel fantastic!'

Kimberley McDowall (9)
Bordon Junior School, Bordon

The Beach At Swanage

At the beach the waves crashed into the rocks calming my mind,
clearing all the bad things.
I felt like dancing with the sea, a salt taste on my lips.
The seagulls were being battered by the wind.
The wind brushing through my hair made me feel like I was in a world
of peace.
I thought to myself I could just lie on the beach and relax.
The blue sea sparkled in the sunlight.
The shells on the beach were washed up and ready to collect.

Jake Black (11)
Bordon Junior School, Bordon

Space Kennings

Night seeker
Fire streaker
Sunset stroller
Endless roller.

Round spinner
Never thinner
Midnight creeper
Falling deeper

Olympic sprinter
Ghostly getter
Fierce fighter
Silver lighter

Shape shifter
Midnight lifter
Silent singer
Great winner.

Tori Coltart (11)
Conifers Primary School, Weymouth

Lunar

Day-sleeper
Night-waker

Stars-neighbour
Space-lover

Changing-phaser
Street-lighter

Light-snatcher
Sun-blocker

Ghostly-glower.

Hannah Palmer (11)
Conifers Primary School, Weymouth

Panic On The Moon

Left alone on the moon
Surrounded by misty dust
Shooting stars whooshing past
So close, so cold.
          So alone!

Natalie Atkinson (11)
Conifers Primary School, Weymouth

The Gloomy Night

A gloomy night
A gloomy day
The skyscraper comes
Run away.

Chloe Bagwell (11)
Conifers Primary School, Weymouth

Space Invaders

In the middle of the night
Aliens approaching under the moonlight
When aliens take over night
Space ships crash suddenly
Ghostly galleons are sent out
To haunt out trespassers
Not a soul has come back.

Rebecca Bestwick (11)
Conifers Primary School, Weymouth

Aliens

Red and tiny bloodshot eyes
Green and slimy skin
Long yellow fingernails
Bright red, short, dusty hair
Brown and long skinny ears
And golden rotted teeth.

Roxanne Cummins (11)
Conifers Primary School, Weymouth

Dark Space

When I hear the black hole screeching
It sends a tingle down my spine
Am I going to be next?
Sucking its prey into its arms of fires
With long, yellow fingernails
Spitting out screaming people.

Carley Nash (11)
Conifers Primary School, Weymouth

Alien Invasion

He comes to kill
Who steps on his land
He'll slice them up
And bury them in the sand.

He takes a life
Once a day
He uses his evil eyes
To bring out rays.

That will slice them up
He'll take them away
And if they don't get buried
He'll hide them in the clay.

Joshua King (11)
Conifers Primary School, Weymouth

Space

Giant heater
Night creeper

Red planet
Rhymes with Janet

Big rocks
Coco Pops

Ball of fire
Spins on a wire

Light hogger
Steaming rocker.

Ian Ansell (11)
Conifers Primary School, Weymouth

Something In The Ship

The night was gory and gruesome
I felt something was following me
I saw his reflection in the window
His eyes were spooky and scary
I turned and saw a trail of slime
And then I fell
I felt like I was being dragged
I knew this was it
This was the end.

Daniel Bill (11)
Conifers Primary School, Weymouth

The Alien Goddess

She orders her brood to crawl into spaceships and steal a life or two
When they leave, we can smell gas leaking and the room fills with
steam
Crashing down at the speed of light, dripping with blood we lay on
the floor -
Slowly fading away
Our bodies will lie in space forever.

George Cunningham (11)
Conifers Primary School, Weymouth

Night Flasher

Night flasher
Morning dasher
Space hopper
Street lighter
Night hopper.

Andrew McNulty (11)
Conifers Primary School, Weymouth

Space Invaders

In the middle of the night
The ghostly creepers come out
To steal a life from trespassers
Who could it be, what can I say?

We don't know
Everyone we sent has never come back,
Finally ghostly aliens have been *executed*
No more to be found.

Stefenee Grove (11)
Conifers Primary School, Weymouth

Aliens On Pluto!

Aliens were swimming in a river of fresh blood and sweat on the dark,
gloomy planet of Pluto.
A head pops out in the river of doom
There were screams and shouts on Pluto
Suddenly . . .
> *Smash!*
> Pluto is gone . . .

Hazel Pritchard (11)
Conifers Primary School, Weymouth

Time Is Running Out

Looking at the black hole
Running out of oxygen
My lungs feel like bombs inside me
The black hole sucking out all my energy.

James Rosser (11)
Conifers Primary School, Weymouth

Space Planet

On the dusty, forbidden planet
I hear a high-pitched scream
Everywhere I step there's sticky slime
Is it a curse in a dead man's eye?
It steals a life or two
Death's knocking at my door waiting for a reply
I see a quick flash of grey whiz by
My soul in agony
Is this the end for me?

Jack Hoskins (11)
Conifers Primary School, Weymouth

Aliens

A river of green alien blood
L ast night no living soul survived
I   saw one thousand dead aliens floating
E very dagger around was killing all the stars
N o one was there to witness it except
S melly dead bodies.

Jasmine Lonsdale (11)
Conifers Primary School, Weymouth

Hungry

Hearing the black hole moaning, it's hungry for its prey
Needs to eat spacemen, it needs to eat them all.
Still hungry, needs to eat more
Like a hoover sucking food into its arms until there's nothing left at all.

Joe Liggitt (11)
Conifers Primary School, Weymouth

Aliens 2005

I didn't know what was there
But there was something on the playground
In a terrifying thunderstorm.

The aliens falling from space
Very little are they.

But when they touch our Earth
The evolve to big aliens.

As the sun comes out and
All the tiny aliens disappear
Into thin air.

Sophie Hillier (11)
Conifers Primary School, Weymouth

Strange Planet

The foggy planet
Staring in front of me
Smells like rotten eggs
All bodies dead from no oxygen
Rotting away
Planet so cold
Feels like I'm going to die.

Christopher Edwards (11)
Conifers Primary School, Weymouth

Scared

Lying on a planet
Strapped to the floor
With aliens standing over you
Frightened to death
Thinking they're about to kill you.

Aston Butcher (11)
Conifers Primary School, Weymouth

A Green Alien

It was a dark, gloomy night
And nothing was in sight
It's so cold, cold, cold
I'm going blue in the face.

No lift. No spaceship. Nothing
It's getting so scary.
As the stars shine bright.

Funny noises from behind
And what do I find?
One green alien.

Jade Marie Newman (11)
Conifers Primary School, Weymouth

Fear

F is for fright, scaring people away
E is for electric storms bringing fear to the world
A is for *aaahh!* While people run away
R is for running away to someone who can help

O is for oh no my worst fear is here
H is for help, help me from fear

N is for nothing is worse than fear
O is for opposite things from good and happiness

 I is for in danger of fear
M is for 'mum, help me!'

S is for scary things of fear
C is for carrying on with your life after fear
A is for amazing sights of fear
R is for racing away from fear
E is for electronic robots chasing you away
D is for dead people coming back to give you fear.

Darren Minton (8)
Hatch Warren Junior School, Basingstoke

Fear

Fear is when
You're nervous
Fear is when
Your heart is fast
Fear is when
You're scared
Fear is when
Your muscles are tense
Fear is when
The ghosts go *boo!*

You're afraid
Of a skeleton raid
You're afraid
Of a zooming zombie
You're afraid
Of the mummy's curse
But I'm not afraid
Of a tiny mouse!

Philip Christie (8)
Hatch Warren Junior School, Basingstoke

Fear

F is for fear, which sends a shiver down your spine
E is for everyone, dreaming happy dreams
A is for howling all night through
R is for romping monsters

F is for fright, spooking people out
R is for rats, squeaking in the sewers
O is for owls, hooting in the night
M is for measly, Mummy's getting up

T is for trees, swaying in the night
H is for horror, scaring people away
E is for electric, hitting the land

D is for dark, covering the earth
A is for anything crawling through the dark
R is for rain, all coming in a downpour
K is for keyhole, make sure it's locked!
N is for night time, so cold and dark
E is for envious, be envious about the night
S is for someone, creeping in your house
S is for scream, screaming in the dark!

Katie Mahoney (8)
Hatch Warren Junior School, Basingstoke

From My Window

From my window
I can see
Bees buzzing amazingly

From my window
I can see
Snails slivering slowly

From my window
I can see
Children playing gratefully

From my window
I can see
Rabbits hopping
Round a tree.

Tom Mitchell (7)
Hatch Warren Junior School, Basingstoke

Fear At Night

F is for fear coming from under my bed
E is for electrified when you're terrified of ghosts
A is for air swaying around you
R is for *roar!* When a lion roars at me

A is for air swaying all around me
T is for terrified of ghosts

N is for night when the wildlife comes out
I is for insects crawling up my leg
G is for *grr!* When a wolf glares at me
H is for *help!* When I hear it from the forest
T is for terrified when I'm terrified of ghosts.

Carla Russell (8)
Hatch Warren Junior School, Basingstoke

My Fear Poem

Shivering in my shoes
I cautiously crept downstairs
Fear of the monster downstairs
I put my back against the wall
I only wish I had a ball
I wish I could crawl back
But he had a big stack
He got locked in the cupboard
I was very stubborn
I opened the door
And I saw the creep
He tried to grab me
But I said,
'Leave me be!'

Jessica Brady (8)
Hatch Warren Junior School, Basingstoke

Sun And Rain

S izzling sun in the sky so high
U p in day and down at night
N ot a single switch on your TV

A lways out in the sun and no more school
N o more sun and it's back to rain
D on't go out or you will catch a cold

R ain again the plants will grow
A TV will cut out again
I wish the sun was out again
N ow it's pouring into action.

Arron Chapman (8)
Hatch Warren Junior School, Basingstoke

This Is Why You Get Scared Stiff

F ear is the worst thing to feel
E verything I imagine seems so real!
E verything is black and dark
L ices crawling up my back

T errible things inside the word fear
H ungry for your blood
E verything nasty, inside the word fear!

F eeling someone lurking above your head
E verything around seems so wrong
A s soon as it's daylight it will all be gone
R unning away from things you cannot escape

Fear makes your flesh creep and your blood run cold
It is petrifying and you are . . .
Panic-stricken!

Tayla Boote (8)
Hatch Warren Junior School, Basingstoke

Fear

F is for fear creeping around
E is for an ear listening to fear
A is for animals listening
R is for the trees rustling

P is for people not sleeping
O is for people going, 'oh no!'
E is for ear listening to fear
M is for mean people doing fear
S is for spiders creepy crawling.

Leah Dorling (8)
Hatch Warren Junior School, Basingstoke

From My Window I Can See

From my window I can see
Workmen working busily
From my window I can see
Trees waving gently
From my window I can see
Slugs slithering slowly
From my window I can see
Children playing loudly
From my window I can see
Flowers growing steadily
From my window I can see
Rain going drip-drop quietly
From my window I can see
Woodpeckers pecking on a tree
From my window I can see
Rabbits jumping round a tree.

Amy Knight (8)
Hatch Warren Junior School, Basingstoke

Fear, Fear

Fear, fear I'm all on my own
Fear, fear no one else home!

Fear, fear I hear strange noises
Fear, fear who could it be?

Fear, fear what shall I do?
Fear, fear I'll sit here quietly!

Fear, fear there's a knock at the door!
Fear, fear who could it be?

Fear, fear who shall I call?
Fear, fear I stand up and quake

Fear, fear I slowly open the door!
Fear, fear it's just my . . . *dad!*

Kayleigh Welton (8)
Hatch Warren Junior School, Basingstoke

A Poem To Be Spoken Silently

(Inspired by Pie Corbet)

It was so silent that I heard
The whisper of the cloud
As it passed by

It was so peaceful that I heard
The grass call
Just before the thunder came

It was so quiet that I could hear
The books screaming
As they were squished into the bookcase

It was so silent that I heard
The sigh of the pencil
Because it was used too much.

Kerry-Anne Jacobs (11)
Kempshott Junior School, Basingstoke

Deep In A Dragon's Lair

(Inspired by Wes Magee's 'Up On The Downs')

Deep in a dragon's lair
Deep in a dragon's lair

Fires fiercely blazed
Mighty dragons destroyed souls
Buildings completely razed
Creatures shivered in the dark hole

Deep in a dragon's lair
Deep in a dragon's lair

Never think you're safe from the dragon's glare!

Harry Rudge (10)
Kempshott Junior School, Basingstoke

Alone In The Dark!

Alone in the dark
Alone in the dark
As the spirits creep
You dart out of sight
The dead bodies weep
The storm stirs up fright
Alone in the dark
Alone in the dark
A high-pitch noise
Like a scream in the park

Down by the river
Down by the river
The poppies blaze
The river flows
As a twisty maze
A maze which grows
Down by the river
Down by the river.

Ryan Johnson (11)
Kempshott Junior School, Basingstoke

Alone In The Dark

(Inspired by Wes Magee's 'Up On The Downs')

Alone in the dark
Where mist covers your shoes
And hides the shadows of the night
Something suddenly moves
An owl in flight
Alone in the dark
Alone in the dark
Cats' eyes glow in front of me like
Ghosts of the night.

Ryan Burn (11)
Kempshott Junior School, Basingstoke

The Tree

The tree sways this way and that
Feeling the wind blowing
He giggles as it tickles his face
He shivers and shudders as squirrels run up and down his back
Collecting nuts and massaging him

He screams with laughter
As the bugs slither and crawl over his leaves and bark

He cries out for help as lighting scorches him
Cooking him to a crisp
The wind and the rain sting him
Like ice cracking on his gnarled branches
He stands thinking about years gone by
And a tear comes to his eye
And when it drops a new tree begins to grow
Day after day he stands there
Wondering if he will be there forever
Or will he be gone before he gets a chance to say goodbye?

Kayleigh Moseley (11)
Kempshott Junior School, Basingstoke

The Tree

The tree screams in pain
As the lighting strikes his bark
His roots clench the ground
As the wind tries to pull him out
The squirrels scuttle up his branches
As he moans and wriggles
The ants crawl up his roots
As he breathes and tries to shake them off.

Danielle Tregent (10)
Kempshott Junior School, Basingstoke

The Bear

The bear, strong and fierce
Will not let anything get in his way
He is powerful and quick, like a cat
Always hungry
Catching his prey he watches, waiting, then all of a sudden . . .
Snap!
The slippery wet fish is like butter in his paws
He grabs it in his sharp ravenous teeth
He savours every bite, as if it were gold
He wanders away in hope of finding some company
No such luck
He ambles to the safety and comfort of his den
To doze in a long and comfortable sleep
Bang! A poacher has killed a poor, defenceless deer
The bear awakes. Angry!
He heaves himself to his feet and lumbers out of his den
The poacher spots him
Shoots him
Once, twice, three times
The bear collapses in a heap on the ground.

Emily Noakes (11)
Kempshott Junior School, Basingstoke

Climbing An Oak Tree

(Inspired by Wes Magee's 'Up On The Downs')

Climbing an oak tree
Climbing an oak tree
A squirrel scatters
It's getting dark
An owl flutters
Lovers kiss and leave their mark
Climbing an oak tree
Climbing an oak tree
The mighty oak is a mansion
Where night creatures flee.

Miles Pope (11)
Kempshott Junior School, Basingstoke

The Magic Box

(Inspired by 'The Magic Box' by Kit Wright)

I will put in the box . . .

The goldest riches of all time
The gentlest rays of the sun at dusk
Fire from the mouth of a red monstrous dragon

I will put in the box . . .

The magic from a wizard's mighty wand
A shepherd taming a bull
A bull tamer herding sheep

I will put in the box . . .

A bottle with Egypt's greatest wonders inside
The dustiest road leading to the Grand Canyon
A sip of crystal clear water, chilling and refreshing

I will put in the box . . .

A swim in a hot spring on a cold winter's day
A yellow moon and a silver sun
The box is my rollercoaster thrilling and fun
A box I can enjoy, when I'm feeling down.

Tom O'Hanlon (11)
Kempshott Junior School, Basingstoke

Alone In A Rockpool

(Inspired by Wes Magee's 'Up On The Downs')

Alone in a rockpool
Alone in a rockpool
Crabs sink into sand
Shrimps dart silently
Urchins wave their hands
Waves crash violently
Alone in a rockpool
Alone in a rockpool
The sun glistens
Like a diamond jewel.

Wayne Collins (11)
Kempshott Junior School, Basingstoke

The Crocodile

The fast, green, scaly monster
Is waiting still, silent
In the tranquil lake
Watching, waiting, wilfully
Creeping up on a buffalo
Like a silent owl at flight
He strikes, quickly, sharply
Taking it into its chainsaw jaws
Death rolling, devouring it down
Where it lay in the monsters stomach
Along with all the other victims remains
Then the monster, again waited, still, silent
In the tranquil lake
Watching, waiting.

Emma Smith (11)
Kempshott Junior School, Basingstoke

The Tree

Waking up the tree stretches to catch the morning sunlight
Wondering if the landscape around him will change today
Laughing as the ants form a chain mountaineering to his leaves
Flinching as the ants swipe leaves from his branches
Like hairs from a head
Bracing himself as the storm clouds approach
Trying hard to dig in his roots as his leaves start to rustle
Yelling, trying to alert the dozing trees around him
As lightning strikes everywhere
Crying after the storm
Tears falling for some of the birds in his branches
And his closest friend who was hit by lightning
Then resting before beginning to re-grow his lost branches.

Christopher Hanson (11)
Kempshott Junior School, Basingstoke

The Magic Box

(Inspired by 'The Magic Box' by Kit Wright)

I will put in the box . . .
The sound of the breeze on the sea
The breath of the last sea lion
The warmth of a bed on a winter's morning

I will put in the box . . .
A snowman with a glowing heart
A dog's smile for the first time
The first and last sunsets

I will put in the box . . .
The dark threat of a crocodile's eyes
The fun of a child's treehouse
The last drop of a waterfall

I will put in the box . . .
My last and first ever piece of writing . . .

Alex May (11)
Kempshott Junior School, Basingstoke

The Tree

The tree's branches scream as lightning strikes them
His trunk laughs as ants crawl up to it
He feels proud as children pick him for their treehouse
But shouts angrily when branches are torn off by those who are careless
He shakes as his brother is chopped down by lumberjacks
He yawns as night approaches after a tiring day of feeling
Animals and people climb through him
He sighs as leaves are torn off by the storm
Then grins as remembers the children he saw
At a younger age
He thinks fondly of times he used to know as he begins to bend.

David Pullar (11)
Kempshott Junior School, Basingstoke

The Magic Box

(Inspired by 'The Magic Box' by Kit Wright)

I will put into the box . . .
The smell of the sea breeze on a cold day
And freshly cut grass in a summer town
The last meal of an ancient pet

I will put into the box . . .
The gentle cry of animals chatting
The crackle of a firework filling the sky with colours
The lapping of the waves rolling onto the beach

I will put into the box . . .
The golden sand shining in the beaming sun
Snowy mountains towering high above the clouds
The glowing lights of a crowded city buzzing
With life in the darkness of midnight

I will put into the box . . .
The soaring heat of the sun beating down onto the beach
The bitterness of the rain drenching to the bone
The warm glow of the lights of the city beating down.

Alex Morley (11)
Kempshott Junior School, Basingstoke

The Bear

He loses his coat in the early summer
He climbs trees all day
He's looking for food at the moment
Honey and fish he will eat
But if you threaten him, he will get you
So watch for the animal with a golden brown coat
Or you might be left
Lying on the floor
Lifeless and still.

Danielle Gill (10)
Kempshott Junior School, Basingstoke

The Magic Box

(Inspired by 'The Magic Box' by Kit Wright)

I will put in the box . . .

The whisper of wind as it brushes past the trees
The great blue ocean that foams and bubbles
With every crashing wave
The sweet perfume of the most delicate rose

I will put in the box . . .

The cool taste of the bluest water, captured in a dream
The eye of the tiger looking for a place of tranquillity
The touch of a baby's hand as she waves hello

I will put in the box . . .

The tip of a mountain covered in fresh, white snow
Falling from the skies
The multicoloured bubbles that float in the air
Then pop into foam
A sigh from a sleeping baby, dreaming in a peaceful dream

I will float on the seven seas, holding my box
Collecting more thoughts and memories.

Phoebe Wright (11)
Kempshott Junior School, Basingstoke

The Elephant

The grasslands of Africa
Hot and dusty, sun beaten barren land
An elephant trudges the desert road
Trunk swinging gracefully, side to side
Tusks point forward, leading the way
His tree trunk legs trample the earth
His ears, like blankets, catch the wind and flap of their own accord
His skin, mud covered, sun dried
Is the bark of a dying tree
He approaches, staring, raises his trunk
And unleashes a thunderous roar.

Hannah Willmott (11)
Kempshott Junior School, Basingstoke

The Magic Box

(Inspired by 'The Magic Box' by Kit Wright)

I will put in the box . . .

A flash of a brilliant firework everlasting
A beautiful memory as bright as day, as colourful as a rainbow
A taste of a golden moon from a faraway universe

I will put in the box . . .

A fifth season with a rainbow sky and a purple river
A snowman with a broken leg slowly dying
A crow soaring through the sky, leaving love and joy behind it.

Ben Pescud (11)
Kempshott Junior School, Basingstoke

I Walk Along

I walk along the cliff top
Crashing waves on the rocks
As men row boats, loggers and cutters
All of a sudden a big knocking on the door
I hear excise men shouting, 'Let us in!'
Horses galloping into the night

I see kegs of brandy being smuggled and excise men going by
The sea clashes with the shore
Old ladies going by, spot lamps shining in front
Smugglers lifting smuggled goods to towers

I feel worried about so many excise men running about
Cold wind blows fast past your face
Scared of a ghost that haunts the graveyard, that people pretended
to be

I feel the coldness of the freezing snow.

Nathaniel Nelson & Luke Watson (11)
Kinson Primary School, Bournemouth

In The Churchyard

I'm creeping through the churchyard
In the dead of night
I'm checking that the coast is clear
It seems to be alright
I tell my crew where they should go
To hide the finest goods
They all go to their places
And do as they should

Our watchman gives his signal
He's seen some people
They're both coming from the pub
One is drunk, the other is humming
We hide the tea and brandy
But not at normal pace
We rush off to be out of sight
We can't be seen in this place

Our ghosts come out to give them a fright
Although they are really girls
But these girls are being paid a price
Their price they request is pearls
Although they're fake they do their job
Those people are really scared
They decide to go and never come again
They now know to beware.

Amy Wareham (11)
Kinson Primary School, Bournemouth

Smugglers Poem

See the ghost come from the churchyard
See the men who think that they are hard
See the 30 kegs of tea being loaded onto a boat
See Issac with his leathered coat
See the moonlight shining down
See the drunken men fall down town
See the darkness surrounding me
See all the fields picked with tea
See all of the horses waiting calmly
Hear Issac and his gang celebrating their success
Hear the waves come crashing up to the sea
Hear the men eating their salmon tea
Hear the devilling silence in the woods
Hear the leaving of the cloaked hoods
Hear the shouting getting near
Hear the smugglers calling in here
Hear all of the trees falling to the ground
Feel the coldness of the air
Feel the wind blowing my hair
Feel the waves on your feet
Feel the sun bring unbearable heat
Feel the swelling of my aching feet
Feel me feeling hungry with meat
Feel the sky enclosing on me
Feel the lightness fighting to see.

Jasmine Gulliver & Cara Dee (10)
Kinson Primary School, Bournemouth

Smugglers

The horses hooves
Are going clip clop
Clip clop, clip clop

There's a chill in the air
As the men go by
Clip clop, clip clop
Clip clop

The excise men are going by
Stop and stand still
Hopefully they won't see us
Clip clop, clip clop

They've just gone past
But they will be back
Now quickly go back
Watch out for that ghost
Clip clop, clip clop, clip clop
Pass them, up to the tower
And hide it
Don't let anyone see you
Clip clop, clip clop, clip clop

The horses hooves
Are going clip clop, clip clop
They are going into the distance
The street has become
Silent again, blow out the candle now
There's no one to be seen around
The time has passed, now go to sleep.

Natasha Fisher (11)
Kinson Primary School, Bournemouth

Smuggler Poem

Hear the waves gently splashing against the boat
The deafening silence of night
The movement of the oars
The fish breaking the surf of the water
The laughter of the crow men

Feel the cold in the air whispering, through the masts
The damp in the sea air
The waves through the wooden boat
The swelling of aching feet

See the moonlight and the stars in the dark blue sky
The moonlight on the waves
The watchmen on the cliffs
The crow on the boat.

Sarah Onions (11) & Leanne Braddock (10)
Kinson Primary School, Bournemouth

Smugglers Bounty

Excise men having a battle
Batman's bat and gunfire
Shooting bullets might hit cattle
Lots of ships, free to hire

Smugglers, sailors, sellers and batmen
Are all on the smugglers bounty
All sheep, cows must have a den
Every smuggler is a bounty

One night a cold breeze
You must have a lot in your backpack
Chilling, cold, you might freeze
Uh-oh, the batman's bat has hit your back.

Josh Cook & Jake Perkin (10)
Kinson Primary School, Bournemouth

Smugglers Poem

Sailing across the sea
Unloading lots of cargo
With 30 tonnes of tea
Very, very tiring though

Be careful of the ghosts
Hearing a big gunshot
Smoking lots of tobacco
Getting really hot

Feel the cold breeze
Slapping your face
Watch out for the excise men
On top of the cliff face.

Connor Threadingham (10) & Dominic Stott (9)
Kinson Primary School, Bournemouth

Langstone Junior School - Haikus

Swimming in year five
Intech visit in year six
Revising for SATs

Weaving in year four
Sewing a hat in year six
Art is so much fun

Miss Fiers in year three
Miss Jacques in year four
Easy work back then

Miss Scott in year five
She was just so hilarious
Miss Mackay to end

Year six is so cool
Teachers help us for tests
Secondary is near.

Samuel Crowe (11)
Langstone Junior School, Portsmouth

Memories

I remember the day I started at school
I'd never thought it would have been this cool
The memories have packed in
Like my head was a box

My friends have all been great to me
When I didn't know how it would be
I don't need to go deep sea
For them to like me to a high degree

There have been lots of lessons
And swimming sessions
The teachers were all kind
They told us to unwind

We went on lots of trips
And the laptops had lots of blips
But our friendship will never rip
Because we won't let it slip.

Lorna Street (10)
Langstone Junior School, Portsmouth

Tornado

Tornado spiral top
Speeding though the town
Deadly objects crashing
Banging, suction
Scared people
Black clouds
Sucking up
Toppling cars
Moving
Swiftly
Tornado
Round
Round.

Bradley Sexton (10)
Langstone Junior School, Portsmouth

Memories Of Langstone

At lunchtime once I got a nasty surprise
I could hardly believe my eyes
I undid my fleece to find
That I'd left my school top behind

When some of us went to Devon
I thought it would be heaven
With half the kids away
We got to run wild and play

Over the years I've had many friends
That ask to borrow rubbers, rulers and pens
Our enormous playground
Is a fun filled fairground

A normal school day
Includes lessons and play
Lunchtimes are fun
We play games and like to run.

Katie Wyatt (11)
Langstone Junior School, Portsmouth

Industrial Panorama

Freezing cold snow falls
Steam coming out of chimneys
People are wrapped up

Hills in the distance
Not many people are outside
It is a cold day

Too much snow around
People indoors by the fire
People on their sleigh.

Craig Richardson (11)
Langstone Junior School, Portsmouth

I Remember

I remember
In year 3
When my teacher was Mr Millross
He screamed, he shouted and he was angry
All day long

I remember
In year 4
When my teacher was Mrs Jones
She didn't tell the other year 4 leaders that she was leaving

I remember
In year 5
When my teacher was Miss Flounders
She was kind of helpful and she never shouted

I still remember
In year 6
My teacher is Mrs Hughes
Mrs Hughes has helped me with everything and also
She is kind to other children
But I will miss every teacher that I have had in the school.

Emily Day (11)
Langstone Junior School, Portsmouth

Year 6 Rap

Listen up I've got something to say
About Langstone School in so many ways
I've had many teachers and lots of friends too
They're really supportive when you're feeling blue
I take many subjects such as P.E.
I find it very interesting and lots of fun too!
My name's Amy Richards
And that's my rap about my school.

Amy Richards (11)
Langstone Junior School, Portsmouth

I Remember

L angstone I will always remember
A nd never forget my first day!
N ow it's time to get ready to leave!
G etting ready to meet new people!
S ATs were very hard, but I survived them!
T ransition work we had to do!
O n Fridays we would had golden time, but not anymore!
N ow I am leaving!
E nough work has been done for me at Langstone!

Jessica Hayward (11)
Langstone Junior School, Portsmouth

My Time At Langstone

L angstone is great
A mazing pupils
N ice teachers
G reat friends
S houting like a thunderstorm
T eachers telling us what to do
O nomatopoeia in literacy
N aughty me
E quilateral in maths.

Paige Graham (11)
Langstone Junior School, Portsmouth

Langstone School

Langstone School is very fun
We get to lay about in the sun
We learn new things nearly every day
And we throw all our complaints away
All the children are extremely good
They're always doing what they should.

Laura Milwain (11)
Langstone Junior School, Portsmouth

Langstone Junior School

Langstone
At the end of Lakeside Avenue
Noisy children
Green and yellow
Scream and shout
Teachers talking
On the playground
No one is quiet until they
Enter the school

Scattering through the school
Children hurry to class
Hours pass on and children get happy
Other times they're not
On the school playground they shout,
'Langstone Junior School!'

Mae Ferrett (11)
Langstone Junior School, Portsmouth

I Remember

It's the end of school
I started off in year 3
Please remember me
There were 3 more years left at school
Only a few more weeks left

I feel really sad
I wish I could never go
But I have to though
Everyone else must feel sad
Now I'm not sad on my own

Off to city, girls
I will not know anyone
But it must be done
We all must go, boys and girls
Please remember me.

Lucy Purcell (11)
Langstone Junior School, Portsmouth

Langstone Junior School

Langstone Junior School
Has always been the greatest
And we are so cool!

With Mrs Hughes and Mr Best
We always work
And get no rest

Langstone Junior School
Has always been the greatest
And we are so cool!

Miss Mackay and Mrs Brown
Have both been kind
And never let us wear a frown

Langstone Junior School
Has always been the greatest
And we are so cool!

Beth Scott (11)
Langstone Junior School, Portsmouth

School Rap

So, listen up I've got something to say
Langstone Juniors is here to stay
Hip hop, bip bop, rap rap

SATS are gone, leavers assembly near
Sports day is every year
Hip hop, bip bop, rap rap

Trips are fun with Beaulieu and Stubbington
But Devon was the best with sheepdogs
Hip hop, bip bop, rap rap

So now you know we're coming to an end
Throughout our 4 years we've been there
Hip hop, bip bop, rap rap.

Rebecca Stockley (10)
Langstone Junior School, Portsmouth

My Memories

On Sports Day
I was glad
Cause we won
That's the best memory I've ever had

Running games
Hopscotch too
The spotless classrooms
And Winnie the Pooh

I remember when
Katie fell in the muck
Everyone laughed
And shouted, 'Tough luck!'

In year five
We all went swimming
We had a race
And I was winning

Now we're in year six
And ready to leave
But I can't believe
How much we've achieved.

Georgia Chandler (11)
Langstone Junior School, Portsmouth

School Poem

School children playing games
Cool
Hungry before lunchtime bell
Annoyed teachers, forgotten homework
Other pupils hyperactive
Lovely lunchtimes fade away.

Bradley Allen (11)
Langstone Junior School, Portsmouth

Langstone Memories

I remember the first day of school
Choke slammed a boy called Jack Woodroofe
My first piece of homework was easy
But I forgot to bring it all

I remember the October
I got detention
Because I ran out the dinner hall
Screaming my head off

I remember November
I was so scared
Because in literacy
There was a firework poem
And I was so scared

I remember the December
I had a birthday
I was really chuffed
Because I had no homework.

Daniel Hardy (11)
Langstone Junior School, Portsmouth

Cool School

School is cool
Naughty kids and clever kids
The teachers are cool

In lessons we learn
Numeracy and science
And literacy

Out to play we go
Children queuing for tuck shop
We are lining up

School is so cool
Naughty kids and clever kids
The teachers are cool.

Jack Woodroofe (10)
Langstone Junior School, Portsmouth

Langstone Memories

My school is like a cake
Enjoyable, welcoming fun
100s and 1000s of memories sprinkled within.

Stress of SATs
Lots of chats
Sports day fun
For everyone

The school is like a swimming pool
Full of water, tears
But we go Mrs Harvey to confront our fears.

Trips away
Games to play
Sketching in art
Science, 'the heart'

The school is like a comedian
Laughing in lessons
What fun they are, I should be left with a laughing scar.

Over the years
I have fun with my peers
But I'm leaving this school
My one and only jewel.

Tamzin Cormican (11)
Langstone Junior School, Portsmouth

Tahitian Landscape

Hot, bright, colourful
Red mountains towering high
Swift breeze, dancing trees
Lovely peaceful place to be
Strolling happily, dreaming.

Chay Pope (11)
Langstone Junior School, Portsmouth

Talented Teachers

Mr Best
Must be blessed
With a fabulous skill
Of teaching a class
And making them pass

Miss Mackay
Blew us away
With her knowledge of maths
Get one wrong
There's a warpath

Mrs Hughes
May blow a fuse
If you confuse
Rhythm and blues
With rap

I wish you were here
Learning Shakespeare
Have no fear
It's only on the other side
Of the hemisphere.

Mark Leighton (11)
Langstone Junior School, Portsmouth

School

If you go to school
You already know
That it's really cool
To the teacher you owe
Years of knowledge
So think about
How it will help you in college.

Joseph Smith (10)
Langstone Junior School, Portsmouth

My School Acrostic

L angstone is great
A dventures happening
N ice school
G olden time is the best
S ome children are friendly
T eachers are really cool
O rdinary
N ever is boring
E vents happening around the school

S ports day is so smart
C onfectionery in the tuck shop
H eartaching
O k and nice
O ver the years I've had some fun
L angstone Junior School.

Brooke Saunders (11)
Langstone Junior School, Portsmouth

I Remember

L angstone was fun
A ll the teachers and friends
N ice staff around the school
G rinning to all
S ister has just come
T o see smile
O n the playground
N ear the field
E veryone being cool

J ordan was a good friend
U nless in a mood
N oisy children in classes
I hate to leave the school
O range christingles went to church
R emember, remember, remember the days.

Floss Pearce (10)
Langstone Junior School, Portsmouth

I Remember

I remember
My first teacher in year three
He was very funny
Mr Millross was his name
Once he sneezed very loud
And made me jump!

I remember
In year four, getting my first
Certificate for getting five merits
I remember . . .
Getting into trouble for something
That I didn't do!

I remember
All my best friends
Emily, Katie R and Naomi
Unfortunately Naomi left
So we don't see each other that much anymore

I remember . . .
Stubbington study centre and Devon
They were great!

Thanks Langstone for giving
Me such a memorable four years!
I will miss you all!
Thank you!

Zoe Martin (11)
Langstone Junior School, Portsmouth

Road Post The View

Winding blue ribbon dock
Distant hills and red throat
A road to the past
I feel alone in this place
Desolate, abandoned.

Amber Haly (11)
Langstone Junior School, Portsmouth

I Remember

L angstone memories
A bout the good times
N aughty kids get in trouble
G rumpy teachers on Friday
S illy kids messing around
T ough teachers
O h it's Mrs Rudgley
N o *not* more homework
E nough homework for once

J udging the teachers as they work
U nusual on a Monday
N ever grumpy on Monday
I like Miss Mackay
O n occasions
R ubbish lessons.

Ashley Helm (10)
Langstone Junior School, Portsmouth

I Remember!

I remember!
R eading my Roald Dahl book
E ating in the school dinner hall for the first time
M rs Feirs, Mrs Jacques, Mrs Scott
E ntering the talent show for the first time
M eeting my first friend Dylan
B eauli's car museum
E ntering the talent show for the second time
R emember me Langstone!

Samuel Wilkin (10)
Langstone Junior School, Portsmouth

I Remember

I remember
R eading with Mr Millross
E very one being friends
M r Millross teaching me
E very one having fights
M rs Jones leaving
B eing very happy
E nd of school is near please
R emember me
A ll my memories of here are still fresh as
T ime passes on and on
L angstone is a good school
A nd is fun
N ot one thing bad except
G etting told off
S tarting school is fun
T oo much sadness
O nly I have to leave
N o one forget me
E very one goodbye.

Jamie Cooper (11)
Langstone Junior School, Portsmouth

Spring

Bumblebees buzzing
Blossoms fresh, wind is blowing
Fresh flowers growing

Flowers are rising
Children playing in the grass
Blossoms on the ground.

Amy Turton (11)
Langstone Junior School, Portsmouth

I Remember

I remember . . .
My first day at Langstone Junior School
Staying close to Mae and Paige
My teacher Mrs Cutler, told us all the rules
About going to a farm

We were told to behave and do not run
But nothing would stop us having fun
Eating our lunch at 12 noon
Unfortunately Mae forget her yoghurt and spoon

I remember . . .
It was time for year 4
To meet Mr Best, he was kind
And great to wind up
Then the Beaulieu trip came
And new friends learnt my name
It was on a farm
But definitely was not calm

I remember in year 5 my teacher Mrs Hughes
Meeting her first class as she was very new
Then I went on a Stubbington trip
On the coach I had a kip
Sharing a bunkbed
And we were all well fed
I remember in year 6
Well all it was *SATs SATs SATs*
But I got through it.

Kate Willis   (10)
Langstone Junior School, Portsmouth

Lunchtime At Langstone

Lunchtime at Langstone are always quite fun
Whether on the field or on the playground
I always find myself running around

Every time the whistle goes
Everyone doesn't want to go in
And if you're playing a game, who's going to win?

Ellen Cooper (10)
Langstone Junior School, Portsmouth

Kangaroo

I see very sharp cactus
Pointy and vicious
I'm scared it might hurt me.

I see smooth sand
Soft and hot
I feel relaxed on it.

I feel the hot heat
Sweating and tired
I want to go to the shade.

I feel my baby in my pouch
Secure and safe
I want my baby to stay with me forever.

I hear the sweet birds chirping
Chirp-chirp-chirp
I want to lay down while they sing.

I hear the sound while I jump,
Slowly and calmly
I want to go and lay down on it suddenly.

Yo Yo Hung (11)
Mill Rythe Junior School, Hayling Island

Love!

Love is the colour of pink and red.
Love sounds like birds singing on a warm summer day.
Love smells like a romantic red rose.
Love feels like a soft, fluffy chick.
Love tastes like warm runny melted chocolate.
Love reminds me of happiness.
Love makes me smiley and happy.

Sasha Heathcote (11)
Mill Rythe Junior School, Hayling Island

Silence

Silence is the colour of white like a plain city.
Silence sounds like a dead graveyard.
Silence smells like water in a cup.
Silence feels like thin air.
Silence tastes like a plain white bun.
Silence reminds me of a deserted playground.
Silence makes me feel plain and dull.

Jack Reynolds (10)
Mill Rythe Junior School, Hayling Island

Love

Love is the colour of red and pink.
Love sounds like birds singing on a beautiful summer's day.
Love smells like a romantic red rose.
Love feels like a soft fluffy chick.
Love tastes like lovely, runny, melted chocolate.
Love reminds me of happiness.
Love makes me feel happy and free.

Chloe Kiellor (10)
Mill Rythe Junior School, Hayling Island

VE Day

What can you see?
Planes are darting and dodging from enemy fire,
Men are falling to their knees without a hope,
Corpses are being taken away,
My friend is now dead,
Fire, fire, fire.

What can you hear?
Machine guns constantly hammering away,
Screams here and there,
The screams are everywhere,
A wounded soldier crying for help,
With no one around,
With no one to care.

What can you feel?
My gun is weighing me down, to the floor,
Also the pain of bullets piercing my side,
Just remember, I'm fighting for life,
And my son, my daughter and my wife.

Luke Spencer (10)
Mill Rythe Junior School, Hayling Island

Soldier In War

I can hear bombs hurting my ears,
Screaming from dying people,
Shouting from soldier.

I feel pain from my friends
Pain from bullets.

I can see guns shooting at me,
Bombs at the shelter.

Yes ten down, but millions to go.

Amy Knight (11)
Mill Rythe Junior School, Hayling Island

A Soldier At War

All can hear is people
Screaming, crying,
And bullets flying.
All I hope for is
To live through this.
All I can see is
Dead people
On the ground
With planes bombing.

Bullets flying over my head.
All I can feel is
Lots of mud on my body
I wish, I wish, I can live
Through this.

Joshua Wood (11)
Mill Rythe Junior School, Hayling Island

The Land Of War

My friends have all been shot,
But the war is still going on,
I can see a lot of gunshots,
All coming at me.
I can feel the blood,
Trickling down my face,
I can hear shots,
But now nothing else.
I can see, I can see nothing,
All I have now is my touch,
But that will probably be gone,
With my life!

Max Jones (10)
Mill Rythe Junior School, Hayling Island

World War One

I can hear the gun shots,
I can feel the coldness of the wind,
All my friends are dead now,
I can feel the blood on my hands,
It will not go away,
I don't want to be here,
I want to be back home,
That's where I belong,
I'm not tough enough to be here,
I'm getting really scared,
More people are,
Every single day,
The gun shots are getting louder,
We're getting really close,
It's so quiet now,
I think I'm going deaf,
'Bang' the pain rushing through my body,
'Bang' I've been hit again,
I'm holding onto my gun and strength,
'Bang' yes got him back,
But now it's all going black,
I'm gone.

Ashley Reynolds (11)
Mill Rythe Junior School, Hayling Island

Anger

Anger is red like the blood of a wounded soldier,
Anger smells like ash and lava from a recently erupted volcano.
Anger feels like a bomb exploding in your mind.
Anger tastes like chillies burning your tongue.
Anger reminds me of fire destroying houses.
I react to anger by lashing out like a king cobra.

William Ellis (10)
Mill Rythe Junior School, Hayling Island

The Rainforest

What can you see?
Monkeys swinging from tree to tree,
Elephants parading through the forest,
Ants are scampering around the dusty ground,
Snakes slithering through the vines.

What can you hear?
Parrots chirping their little song,
Frogs are croaking their tunes,
The howl of a howler monkey echoing through the forest,
Beautiful birds are tweeting.

What can you feel?
I feel warm and relaxed,
The best place to be.

Melody Kwiatkowski (11)
Mill Rythe Junior School, Hayling Island

Happiness

Happiness is red like a big red rose
Happiness is sweet and calm like
Soft sand sliding through your hand
Happiness smells like sweet and sour
Chicken with egg fried rice
Happiness feels like laying in your bed
Dreaming of Christmas coming to your door
Happiness tastes like McDonald's wrapped in a bun
Happiness reminds me of good times I've had with my
                                        best friends.
Happiness makes me feel like singing in my garden
On a hot summer's day.

Charlotte Sinden (10)
Mill Rythe Junior School, Hayling Island

Environment

Environment is precocious,
Fumes fling out the exhaust of cars,
The motorist can feel the big fat handlebars with his hands,
He can feel the hot engine with his legs,
He can hear the engines of other cars,
He can hear dogs barking in the park,
He can even hear cats miaowing,
He can see pavement, silver pavement,
He can see trees, green trees,
He can see houses, brick houses,
Environment is as precocious as me.

Dogs can see balls,
Dogs can see cars,
Dogs can see people playing,
Dogs can hear cars,
Dogs can hear football players shouting,
Dogs can hear their owners saying, 'Come here boy,'
Dogs can feel the long smooth grass on their feet,
Dogs can feel the ball in their mouth.

The lady can see children in the park,
The lady worrying what will happen to her child,
The lady seeing cars going down the road,
The lady hearing children shouting and crying by falling off the slide,
The lady hearing cars zooming down the road,
So be careful in and around the park.

Shane Day (11)
Mill Rythe Junior School, Hayling Island

Love

Love is like a pillow filled with feathers.
Love is like two doves flying in the sky.
Love is a rose filled with chocolate.
Love is like a bond with a friend.
Love is like your friends and family.

Benjamin Diment (11)
Mill Rythe Junior School, Hayling Island

Mask Poem

I see people staring at me, looking at my expressions.
I hear people laughing at me making silly noises while
I'm being transformed to a head shape.
I don't know what I look like but it must be bad, I hope not.
I begin to get drier as the day goes on.
I wonder what accessories they are going to put on me,
Hoping they will be pretty.
Most days my breakfast, lunch and dinner are little bits of
Sticky glue from the brown tape, they put on me repetitively.

Emma West (11)
Mill Rythe Junior School, Hayling Island

Hate

Hate is as red as red wine,
Hate sounds like a teacher groaning on a rainy day,
Hate smells of flint freshly rubbed together,
Hate feels like a fist punching your best friend,
Hate reminds me of getting into fights with friends,
I walk away from hate.

Jack Watts (11)
Mill Rythe Junior School, Hayling Island

Happy John

I am a happy mask with my mask friends.
I'm not scared of other masks.
I am being painted with yellow and black making up my face.
I was painted with a smile just as I wanted.
I will always look on the bright side even when hurt.

Luke Rigden (11)
Mill Rythe Junior School, Hayling Island

The Tropical Bird

I wake to see the morning sun,
An armadillo near my nest.
It scurries off and then I hear,
The leopard's morning growl.

I stretch my wings and then I feel,
The wind blowing through my feathers,
Then I set off through the sky,
To find my berry breakfast.

I see crocodiles lying low,
And bats going straight to bed.
I hear Toucans calling from below,
And parrots flying overhead.

I hear snakes slithering and sliding
Through the leaves,
Ready to pounce on their prey.
I hear the pitter-patter of the rain,
Falling on the leaves.

I eat my meal then go to bed,
The sun has gone, and that's my song.

Peter Thomas (11)
Mill Rythe Junior School, Hayling Island

Love

Love is like a soft, pink cloud floating in the sky.
Love is like an angel singing a soft melody
From the heavens above.
Love smells like the ocean's breeze blowing in your face.
Love tastes like a tube of ice cream melting on your tongue.
Love reminds me of good without bad.
Love makes me feel warm inside.

Stephen Newman (11)
Mill Rythe Junior School, Hayling Island

A Tree In A Rainforest

What can you see?
Hairy, eight-legged freaks, scuttling around ready to devour
their prey.
Dark, grey, rigid clouds lurking ready to explode.
Distant villages with thatched roofs, going up in flames as a
bush fire spreads.
Young, fluffy, brown monkeys swinging from tree to tree.

What can you hear?
Aquatic blue streams, racing down a sloped hill lined with
Mangrove trees.
City hunters and their guns, aiming, firing and killing.
Rainforest tribes gathered for a meeting, doing a strange
singing ceremony.
Suspicious and scary rustling, makes all the animals alert.

What can you feel?
Cool, cold drizzle, trickling down my neck, sending a shiver down
my spine.
Lime green insects inspecting a part of me.
A cold, hard stabbing pain, as animals drop dead.
Small smiles that are shared by mother animals,
As their young leave them alone.

Hannah Darbey (11)
Mill Rythe Junior School, Hayling Island

St Lucia

I can feel the wind blowing.
I can hear the children playing.
I can see the golden sand glittering in the sun.
I can hear the sea crashing.
I can see people swimming and splashing.
I can feel the heat burning me.

Kimberley Dean (11)
Mill Rythe Junior School, Hayling Island

Silence!

Silence is white like a puddle of melted snow.
Silence sounds like no one is there.
Silence smells cold like all the windows are open.
Silence feels sad like a child crying.
Silence tastes like water.
Silence reminds me of death.
Silence makes me feel alone.

Adrienne Francis-Robertson (11)
Mill Rythe Junior School, Hayling Island

Darkness

Darkness is the colour of black in a midwinter's night.
Darkness sounds silent because nothing is moving.
Darkness smells like smoke from a chimney.
Darkness tastes like fear on a scary night.
Darkness reminds me of people being murdered in the moonlight.
Darkness means I hide under my duvet.

Joe Barber (11)
Mill Rythe Junior School, Hayling Island

Fear

Fear is black like exploding ink,
Fear sounds like horrified children screaming in the dark,
Fear smells like sausages burning on a barbecue,
Fear feels like dusty smoke running through your fingers,
Fear tastes like spicy curry burning in your mouth,
Fear reminds you of a scary movie such as in The Ring,
Fear makes you react with steam bursting out your ears.

Jodie Morgan (11)
Mill Rythe Junior School, Hayling Island

A Soldier At War

Lo: To write a descriptive poem in a given format.

What can you see?
I can see bombs shattering,
Blowing towns apart,
Lots of dying, by people being shot,
Countries being torn a lot.

What can you hear?
I can hear tanks rolling into battle,
Shaking everyone in sight,
Bodies falling to the ground,
It's too blurry, too much sound.

What can you feel?
A shiver running up my back,
It's putting me off the battle,
I want to return home,
Everyone's dead, I'm alone.

Lisa Haines (11)
Mill Rythe Junior School, Hayling Island

Happiness

Happiness is red like a big red rose.
Happiness is sweet and calm like soft sand going through
                                    your hands.
Happiness smells like sweet and sour chicken with rice,
And vanilla ice cream mixed up with cream as a drink.
Happiness feels like laying in your bed fast asleep, dreaming
About Christmas coming to your door.
Happiness tastes like McDonald's in a bun.
Happiness reminds me of the good times I have had with my friends.
Happiness makes me feel like singing in the rain, or wind,
On a hot summer's day.

Samantha King (11)
Mill Rythe Junior School, Hayling Island

War

What can you see?
Dead bodies scattered around the streets,
The soldiers that risked their lives, made the town bloody,
Tanks destroying rotten old buildings,
A deadly bullet flashing quickly past my head.

What can you hear?
Soldiers marching into battle, fighting for their country,
The rattling of a machine gun,
Bombs being dropped, destroying warriors' lives.
The terror of a frightened soldier being killed.

What can you feel?
It's my first time in a war, I feel nervous.
Black skies surround this town, it's making me feel cold.
I feel frightened with bullets flying around.
I'm fighting for my family, I can't be scared.

Matthew Blackburn-Smith (11)
Mill Rythe Junior School, Hayling Island

Sandy Beach

The hot sun burning on your body,
The breeze of a gentle wind,
The sand running through your fingers,
And the cold ice from your drink.

You hear the children playing,
Running in the sand,
The adults are relaxing,
While the sun fades away.

You see the palm tree swaying,
Gently from the wind,
People start to leave,
As the beach empties again.

Lauren Pratt (11)
Mill Rythe Junior School, Hayling Island

Child In The Playground

What can you see?
A child on their own, sitting by a tree,
Trees in a clump, swaying in the breeze,
A ball of bronze, not trying its best,
And rain on the roof, pouring down.

What can you hear?
The laughter of children having fun,
Birds in trees, chirping and singing,
Rain on the roof, pouring down,
And boys playing football, running around.

What can you feel?
Sadness, being spread around
Weakness, coming from the heart,
Being lonely, all the time,
I hate life, it's so unfair.

Tasha Jeal (10)
Mill Rythe Junior School, Hayling Island

Happiness

Happiness is like a pink flower.
Happiness a like a colourful butterfly.
Happiness is like a green, pink, purple rainbow.
Happiness is red like a red rose.
Happiness is sweet and calm like soft sand
Sliding through your fingers.
Happiness smells like sweet and sour chicken
With vanilla flavoured ice cream.
Happiness feels like laying in your bed,
Dreaming of Christmas coming to your door.
Happiness tastes like a McDonald's wrapped in a bun.
Happiness reminds me of good times I have had with my friends.
Happiness makes me feel like singing in the rain on cold or hot
summer days.

Kate Hinsley (10)
Mill Rythe Junior School, Hayling Island

Happiness

Happiness is yellow like the burning sun.
Happiness sounds like birds singing when the sun is rising.
Happiness smells like fresh baked bread coming out of the oven.
Happiness feels like the hot sun burning on my back.
Happiness tastes like chocolate melting on my tongue.
Happiness reminds me of children playing in the sea splashing
All about, all around.
Happiness makes me react all warm and loved.

Jemma Byron (11)
Mill Rythe Junior School, Hayling Island

Happiness

Happiness is orange like a happy boiling sun,
Happiness is laughter bouncing through the land.
Happiness is soft chocolate melting on your tongue,
Happiness is sweet with a hint of mint,
Happiness is full of smiles jumping around,
Happiness is wobbly like melting ice cream,
Happiness reminds me of my family and friends and
How much love the world shares.

Maisie Green (11)
Mill Rythe Junior School, Hayling Island

Happiness

Happiness is a golden yellow like the sun beaming down,
Happiness sounds like the sweet melody of a bird in the early hours
of the morning,
Happiness tastes like a luscious, tasty sensation,
Happiness is a colourful flower blooming for all to see,
Happiness feels delicate and soft like the finest silk carefully
woven together,
Happiness reminds me of a bright, summer's day where the grass
Is swaying from side to side.

Roxanne Scott (11)
Mill Rythe Junior School, Hayling Island

Love

Love is pink like candyfloss from a trip to the fair,
Love is like champagne trickling down a wine glass,
Love is the first sight of a glistening rainbow,
Love is like a hand-picked rose petal,
Love looks like a fluffy kitten, small and sweet,
Love is a moment that erases sadness and worries forever,
Love reminds me of a heart beating rhythmically.

Loren Jones (11)
Mill Rythe Junior School, Hayling Island

Anger

Anger is red like a brewing fire,
Anger is a lion roaring at its prey,
Anger smells like petrol leaking from a car,
Anger is like a sour lemon,
Anger is like a monster ready to pop out of its hole,
Anger reminds me of when my step dad died.

Dale Cooper
Mill Rythe Junior School, Hayling Island

Fear

Fear is a black carpet of blindness,
Fear is an evil clown's laugh,
Fear is the bitter taste of blood,
Fear has the foul stench of rotting flesh,
Fear is a red eyed clown's murderous smile,
Fear has the texture of a Tarantula's hairy legs,
Fear reminds me of a film I once saw.

William Nelson (11)
Mill Rythe Junior School, Hayling Island

Love

Love is pink like flowers grazing in a field,
Love sounds like a baby's laughter echoing throughout a distant land.
Love tastes like a ripe strawberry.
Love smells like a sweetly scented flower,
Love looks like a rainbow glistening in the sky,
Love feels like silk, soft and smooth,
Love reminds me of a single red rose,
Giving out its wonderful scent.

Jay Matthews (10)
Mill Rythe Junior School, Hayling Island

Happiness

Happiness is blue like the summertime sky,
Happiness is the singing of the birds,
Happiness is sweet like freshly picked strawberries.
Happiness is the fresh air around us,
Happiness is bright and cheerful faces in the sunlight,
Happiness is the soft fur of newborn kittens,
Happiness reminds me of when I first saw my kitten, Storm.

Samantha Davies (11)
Mill Rythe Junior School, Hayling Island

Hatred

Hatred is the sound of dogs barking and growling,
Hatred is a pit of never-ending darkness,
Hatred is burning wood giving off shed loads of black smoke,
Hatred is hot chillies burning in your mouth,
Hatred is fire burning your hand,
Hatred reminds me of fire burning freely.

Zach William-Wright (11)
Mill Rythe Junior School, Hayling Island

A Tree In The Rainforest

What can you see?
I can see colourful birds stretching their wings
I can see the rain that is hitting everything
I can see different coloured flowers that have the greatest smells
I can see bluebells that really look like bells.

What can you hear?
I can hear a leopard yawning trying to sleep
I can hear the sea waves crashing, which are so deep
I can hear rain pouring onto the leaves
I can hear creatures rushing that look like thieves.

What can you feel?
I can feel creatures crawling up me
I can feel monkeys sitting down then jumping to different trees
I can feel the rain hitting me and everything in its way
I can feel the sun burning me with its rays.

Yasmine Farbrace (11)
Mill Rythe Junior School, Hayling Island

Happiness

Happiness is yellow like the bright sun giving joy in all of its light.
Happiness sounds like birds singing cheerfully in the morning
of spring.
Happiness tastes like a sweet cookie fresh out of the hot oven.
Happiness smells like colourful flowers gazing at the sunlight.
Happiness looks like a rainbow, vivid and cheerful.
Happiness feels like soft silk rubbing against your skin.
Happiness reminds me of laughter and fun.

Ben Lawrence (10)
Mill Rythe Junior School, Hayling Island

Love

Love is the colour of a fresh grapefruit,
Love is a harp playing in your soul,
Love is a pink candyfloss,
Love is a red rose melting in your heart,
Love is a feeling you can't let go of
Love feels like a feeling you never felt before,
Love reminds me of freshly picked flowers in the garden.

Emily Hammond (11)
Mill Rythe Junior School, Hayling Island

Love

Love is red like a beating heart,
Love sounds like a harp playing in your soul,
Love tastes like a sugar cane mesmerising your mind,
Love smells like a lavender aroma from a quality bunch,
Love is a ballroom dancer going with the flow,
Love feels like a feeling never been felt,
Love reminds me of a first kiss.

Chloe Fox-Hoare (10)
Mill Rythe Junior School, Hayling Island

Fear

Fear is dark black, like storm clouds above,
Fear sounds like a girl screaming at night,
Fear tastes like a red hot chilli burning in your mouth,
Fear smells like rotten flesh,
Fear looks like an evil clown with a gun,
Fear feels like the roughness of concrete,
Fear reminds me of a man with a mask on
That I saw when I was little.

Oliver Williams (11)
Mill Rythe Junior School, Hayling Island

A Child In The Playground

What can I see?
Other pupils enjoying themselves, running around having fun,
Young boys playing football, improving their skills,
Children swapping cards, improving their deck,
Running over bumpy hills.

What can I hear?
Birds flying around, singing a wonderful tune,
Children shouting and screaming, having fun,
Talking to their friends, talking about how to do something on a game,
Groups of children argue, not getting along.

What can I feel?
Happy, that children get along,
Pleased, that children playing nicely together,
Not happy, that people are fighting,
Not pleased, that friends are falling out.

Kieran Dyke (11)
Mill Rythe Junior School, Hayling Island

Anger

Anger's colour is dark red,
It sounds like boiling water,
Anger tastes like red hot chillies,
Burning in your mouth.

Anger smells like burning coal,
It looks like a hot fire,
Anger feels like scalding steam,
Rising from the kettle.

Anger reminds me of England losing the World Cup.

Oliver Heath (11)
Mill Rythe Junior School, Hayling Island

Happiness

Happiness is a joyful feeling
Happiness tastes of a sour sweet
Happiness is the colour of yellow like the golden sun
Happiness tastes like a bar of chocolate all for me.

Happiness feels like the soft cotton on my cheek
Happiness sounds like the cheerful children playing in
the summertime
Happiness looks like people on holiday surfing on the sea
Happiness, it reminds me of my best friend.

Harry Hancock (11)
Mill Rythe Junior School, Hayling Island

Anger!

Anger is the colour black triumphing over day
Anger is the sound of a fist slamming on my door
Anger is the taste of a hot pepper melting away my tongue
Anger is the smell of rubber melting in a fierce fire
Anger looks like a dark shadow with a no owner at all
Anger feels like an ice cube trickling down my back
Anger reminds me of the death happening in war right now.

Connor Henry (10)
Mill Rythe Junior School, Hayling Island

Happiness

Happiness is the colour of light pink
Happiness sounds like children laughing and playing
Happiness tastes like a sweet sherbet lemon
Happiness smells like a fresh little daisy
Happiness looks like a sweet blooming pink rose
Happiness feels like soft baby's skin
Happiness reminds me of a big bouncy trampoline.

Nicola Emms (11)
Mill Rythe Junior School, Hayling Island

Happiness

Happiness is pink like a blooming rose
Happiness sounds like a newborn bird singing
Happiness tastes like a soft marshmallow
Happiness smells like a bunch of sweet flowers
Happiness looks like a sun setting on a tropical island
Happiness feels like a soft new blanket
Happiness reminds me of when my family were together.

Rachel Emms (11)
Mill Rythe Junior School, Hayling Island

Happiness

Happiness is the colour of a ripe red rose
Happiness sounds like a sparrow tweeting gently
Happiness tastes so sweet like my favourite chocolate
Happiness smells like a drop of lemon juice fresh in the morning
Happiness looks so bright and colourful like a rainbow
Happiness feels like a soft petal from a daisy rubbing against my face
Happiness reminds me of friendship and how warm it makes me feel.

Sammy Price (11)
Mill Rythe Junior School, Hayling Island

Anger

Anger is red like the colour of blood from a cut wound.
Anger sounds like a scream of fear from an infant.
Anger tastes like a red hot pepper burning in your mouth.
Anger smells like a thick cloud of smoke slowly suffocating.
Anger looks like a terrible tsunami washing families apart.
Anger feels like the heat of a fire burning up inside me.
Anger reminds me of innocent people being murdered.

Katie Harland (11)
Mill Rythe Junior School, Hayling Island

Angry

Angry is like a volcano destroying everything in its path
Angry smells like death from every direction
Angry sounds like crying and misery
Angry looks like steam blasting from a building
Angry tastes like blood everywhere you go
Angry reminds me of the world choosing the path with no good in it.

Bobby Coulter (11)
Mill Rythe Junior School, Hayling Island

Happiness

Happiness is the colour yellow, like the sun sizzling.
Happiness sounds like a million surprises popping up at once.
Happiness tastes like the ripest strawberry, getting ready to
                                        be picked.
Happiness smells of a rosebud just about to open up.
Happiness feels like a warming hug from your mum.
Happiness reminds me of meeting new friends.

Emily Lewis (10)
Mill Rythe Junior School, Hayling Island

Love

Love is a small pink heart.
Love sounds like children playing.
Love tastes like lovely sweets.
Love smells so sweet like melting chocolate.
Love looks like a pony playing in a field.
Love feels like a teddy in your arms.
Love reminds me of sweets and sweet smelling roses.

Charlotte Hensby (11)
Mill Rythe Junior School, Hayling Island

Love

Love is red like a petal of a rose,
Love sounds like an echo from a voice far, far away,
Love tastes like chocolate melting in your mouth,
Love smells like a red, red rose,
Love looks like fluffy, red cotton,
Love feels like sand on a tropical island,
Love reminds me of my kiss.

Jack Reed (11)
Mill Rythe Junior School, Hayling Island

Anger!

Anger is a red devil eating my insides,
Anger is a roaring lion lashing out on me,
Anger is a killer fire burning all of me,
Anger is a tsunami killing everyone,
Anger is a worst nightmare haunting me every day,
Anger is the smell of thick black smoke trying to kill,
Anger is a big lump nobody can swallow.

Annie Godwin (11)
Mill Rythe Junior School, Hayling Island

Love

Love is pink like a baby's face.
Love sounds like loving laughter.
Love tastes like a thick, delicious, white chocolate.
Love smells like a Sunday roast cooking.
Love looks like a paradise island with soft sand and a calm sea.
Love feels like a petal rubbing against your face.
Love reminds me of my grandma and how much she loved and
cared for me.

Jessica Bone (11)
Mill Rythe Junior School, Hayling Island

Sadness

Sadness is black like a closed room,
Sadness sounds like the loud brass band,
Sadness tastes of rotten water in the river,
Sadness smells like a muddy, wet dog,
Sadness looks like a cold roast dinner,
Sadness feels like a cold rainy day,
Sadness reminds me of when my grandad shouts.

Matthew Bird (11)
Mill Rythe Junior School, Hayling Island

Love

Love is blue like the deep sea.
Love tastes of sweet strawberries and chocolate.
Love sounds like the calm sea running up and down the shore.
Love smells of a field of flowers in bloom.
Love feels like a flood of joy.
Love looks like wild dolphins jumping in the sunset.
Love reminds me of a caring family.

Rachel Stanway (11)
Mill Rythe Junior School, Hayling Island

Love

Love is the colour of pink and red.
Love smells like a red, red rose.
Love looks like a sweet strawberry.
Love feels like a soft, comfy cushion.
Love sounds like a child playing happily.
Love tastes like a dreamy chocolate bar about to be eaten.
Love reminds me of a garden of red roses about to bloom.

Kimberley Mackey (11)
Mill Rythe Junior School, Hayling Island

Charlie Heaton

Charlie Heaton is a boy,
Who can really annoy,
He's very thick,
Not that bright,
He'll annoy you day and night!

Charlie Heaton likes to play,
In a very violent way,
He's very thick,
Not that bright,
You can't get past him without a fight!

Charlie Heaton likes to kick,
He also really likes to nick,
He's very thick,
Not that bright,
His weakness is that he can't write!

Charlie Heaton has a gun,
He shoots caps at people just for fun,
He's very thick,
Not that bright,
Beware! He has a vicious bite!

Charlie Heaton's my best friend,
He only lives around the bend,
He's very thick,
Not that bright,
His favourite toy is his big kite.

Charlie Heaton's grown up now,
The good thing is he's no more foul,
He's not that thick,
He's bright,
He's changed a lot since he was a tike!

Harry Grace (8)
Rudgwick Primary School, Rudgwick

My Little Sister

My little sister got a blister in her thumb
She *yelled* for Mum,
But Mum didn't come
She *yelled* some more
And fell onto the floor.
When Mum came
It wasn't the same
The blister had burst
Things got worse
My sister bled and bled
Mum thought she was dead.
Suddenly my sister woke up,
'Mum what's up?'
'But I thought you were dead!'
'Hey Mum, I only bumped my head!'

Sarah Twyford (8)
Rudgwick Primary School, Rudgwick

Animal Menus

Crabs eat kebabs!
Lemurs eat lemons!
Sharks eat sushi!
Lions eat lychees!
Dodos eat dinosaurs!
Spiders eat spears!
Baboons eat bananas!
Sparrows eat soap!
Rats eat rabbits!
Rabbits eat roast!
Frog eats logs!
Scorpions eat sparrows!
Crocs eat crabs.

Kelsey Cairns (8)
Rudgwick Primary School, Rudgwick

Animal Menus

Crocs eat crisps.
Spiders eat spears.
Sparrows eat spades.
Rats eat cats.
Rabbits eat roses.
Dodos eat doughnuts.
Scorpions eat scouts.
Frogs eat pharaohs.
Dogs eat logs.

Ryan Johnson (8)
Rudgwick Primary School, Rudgwick

Art

Hello, I'm Ed and I like art
I think I'm rather smart
I like to use my paintbrush
Sometimes I might rush
I like to use lots of paint
I wish I was like Leo the saint
I like to draw a funny cartoon
I like to draw the sun and moon
Hello, I'm Ed and I like art.

Edward Webb (8)
Rudgwick Primary School, Rudgwick

Banger Racing

Cars crash and skid
The crowd cheers and the cars throw up dust
They tear around like motorbikes
They roll and tumble over
Crash! Bash!

Daniel Botting (8)
Rudgwick Primary School, Rudgwick

Travelling To School

If the playground was a runway,
I would fly to school by plane.

If the staffroom was a station,
I would steam to school by train.

If the classroom was a stable,
I would ride in at a trot.

If the main hall was a harbour,
I would sail to school by yacht.

Rebecca Cornish (9)
Rudgwick Primary School, Rudgwick

Karate

Karate is fast
Karate is fun
Karate is powerful
When you get slapped on the floor
It really stings!
Karate is cool.

Ryan Dunkley (7)
Rudgwick Primary School, Rudgwick

My Hamster

My hamster is so fluffy,
Her eyes are like a star in the night,
She's so brown and she is brown on belly,
And she bites you a lot,
But she bites me a tot.

Amy Brown (8)
Rudgwick Primary School, Rudgwick

My Horse

My horse is eight years old
And covered in gleaming gold,
I sometimes cuddle it in the night
When it's freezing cold!

A year has passed.

My horse is nine years old
And covered in gleaming gold,
I've learned how to canter now,
Around and around in the field now!

A year has passed.

My horse is ten years old
And covered in gleaming gold,
I sometimes take no notice of her,
But she just jumps around and around!

A year has passed.

My horse is eleven years old
And covered in gleaming gold,
I sometimes find out her talent
But she is my lovely horse and wins races just for me!

A year has passed.

My horse is twelve years old
And covered in gleaming gold,
She is right for me,
And that's the way it is going to be.

Sasha Newman (8)
Rudgwick Primary School, Rudgwick

Cats And Dogs

Cats and dogs like eating frogs,
Round, green and squishy
They grow so fat they never get a rat
And they never get to catch each other.

Amy Sayers (8)
Rudgwick Primary School, Rudgwick

Sports!

Skipping is a happy sport
Jumping high and jumping low
Jumping all around the school
I am very happy now.

Football is a happy sport
Kicking high and kicking low
Kicking all around the school
I am very happy now.

Swimming is a happy sport
Diving high and diving low
Diving all around the school
I am very happy now.

Climbing is a happy sport
Grabbing high and grabbing low
Grabbing all around the school
I am very happy now.

I like all these sports
Sports all day, sports all morn
Sports all afternoon as well
I am very, very happy now!

Nadia Dekany (8)
Rudgwick Primary School, Rudgwick

Mrs Flict

Mrs Flict
Is very strict
She is very small and fat
And carries a big baseball bat.

Mrs Flict
Is very dumb
She has a hugely enormous thumb
Surprisingly she does not notice
That she drives a very nice Lotus!

Emily Townsend (9)
Rudgwick Primary School, Rudgwick

Butterflies

I saw some butterflies twirling round and round
Then I saw one fall to the ground
I thought it was dead
But it was on its leaf bed
Then it flew away and all I wanted to say was
      Goodbye!

It flew right back
It gave me quite a fright
Then I had to say
      Goodnight!

I woke up in the morning
Then I started drawing,
Then I remembered about the butterfly
And it made me cry.

So I went outside and cried more
Then the butterfly came back
Then sat on some old sack

    And I never said goodbye!

Jessica Humphreys (8)
Rudgwick Primary School, Rudgwick

My Puppy

My puppy is so brown
She always rolls around
She is so fluffy and so soft
She has five brothers and
Watch out for your fingers
As she bites a lot.

Rebecca Johnson (7)
Rudgwick Primary School, Rudgwick

My Cat

My cat is as stripy as a tiger
My cat is very good at climbing up trees
My black and white cat will not come back
If you don't feed it properly.

Tiffany Allan (8)
Rudgwick Primary School, Rudgwick

My Fat Cat

My cat was so very fat
As big and fat as an elephant
You won't know about it
Because he's on London Bridge.

Ian Etherington (7)
Rudgwick Primary School, Rudgwick

In The Fridge

Ten round slices of ham
Nine fizzy cans of Coke
Eight smelly eggs
Seven mouldy pieces of bread
Six emerald grapes
Five blocks of cheese
Four sour strawberries
Three half eaten cakes
Two frozen biscuits
One delicious jam sandwich, just for me!

Elizabeth Meacher (11)
St Leonard's CE Primary School, St Leonards-on-sea

Animal Poem

Elephants are wrinkly,
Tigers are stripy,
Monkeys are furry,
Dogs are grumpy.

Cats are cuddly,
Crocodiles are snappy,
Fish are silky,
Dolphins are smooth.

Pigs are pink,
Frogs are green,
Sharks are grey,
And cats are ginger.

Megan Barnes (10)
St Leonard's CE Primary School, St Leonards-on-sea

Is It True?

Is it true,
That we can fly to the moon,
Or live on Mars
But go by cars?

Is it true,
That not all people care,
If they have hair,
Some horses have a lot, especially a mare?

Is it true,
That horses live in a stable,
And always have a label,
But they are very able.

Chloe Campbell (11)
St Leonard's CE Primary School, St Leonards-on-sea

Some Mums

Some mums are big, while others are smaller,
Some mums are short, while other are taller,
Some mums are smart, while others are witty,
Some mums are lovely, delightful and pretty,
Some mums are plain and can be such a bore,
Some mums (in bed) snore, snore, snore!
Some mums are perfect,
But others are definitely not fun,
Some mums are plainly a pain for everyone.

Saffron Oliver (11)
St Leonard's CE Primary School, St Leonards-on-sea

Snowy

My name is Snowy,
I'm not very old,
I live in the snow,
But I don't like the cold,
I sleep all alone on a hard icy bed,
And dream that I'm cosy and cuddled instead,
So when you take me home with you
We will be warm and cosy.

Hollie Francis (11)
St Leonard's CE Primary School, St Leonards-on-sea

Love Poem

Roses are red
Violets are blue
No matter what happens
I will love you.

Ronnie Aubrey (11)
St Leonard's CE Primary School, St Leonards-on-sea

The Cat Who Flew

There once was a cat,
Who sat on a bat,
And flew to a faraway land.

He then ate some cheese,
And got stung by some bees,
Then started his own hippy band.

Because of this he got fat,
And decided to flop on a mat,
You couldn't pick him up by hand.

He went to a gym,
And fell in a bin,
Then made a castle of sand.

Then once again the cat,
Sat on a bat,
And flew back home . . . again.

Mark Goodrum (10)
St Leonard's CE Primary School, St Leonards-on-sea

Horses

The smooth white horse galloped across the plain,
The wind blowing in its silky mane,
He galloped on and on and on until he
Got back to where he belonged.

Back in the forest was where he belonged,
He cantered past his stable and further beyond,
The lush green grass waved to and fro,
As he looked he saw a fawn and doe.

Oh how he felt sorry they were lost in the grass,
But when he looked closer he had been stabbed with some glass,
There was nothing he could do to help the poor doe,
So he plodded slowly on into the meadow.

Bethany Ward (11)
St Leonard's CE Primary School, St Leonards-on-sea

Some Babies

Babies come in all shapes and sizes,
Sometimes they come as little surprises,
Some babies are chubby and some are not,
Some babies come with fevers and start to get hot,
Some babies laugh and some babies cry,
Some babies sit and some babies lie,
Some babies are sick and some just dribble,
Some babies chomp and some just nibble,
Whatever the baby they are still cute and soft,
I will still love them all even if I get angry
And chuck them in the loft!

Lily Loughman (11)
St Leonard's CE Primary School, St Leonards-on-sea

One Unlucky Monkey!

There once was a monkey who looked like a king
He had only one problem,
He lived in a bin.

One fine sunny day the bin was removed,
And then put down at the dump,
The bin would get cubed,
Squashed like a 'Frube'.

And the monkey would have more than a bump!
A bump
The monkey would have more than a bump!

Merlin Webster (11)
St Leonard's CE Primary School, St Leonards-on-sea

Simon Cowell Vs Mrs Powell!

Mrs Powell is stressy,
Occasionally her hair is messy,
She yells most of the time,
For her to be nice it must be a crime,
People say that her assemblies are boring,
And that they're almost snoring!

I wonder if Simon Cowell is as bad,
Or if he makes kids mad?
Whether he makes kids cry
Or makes them want to say goodbye?

Well Simon Cowell,
Isn't as bad as Mrs Powell,
He makes people cry,
For their bad singing,
No matter how hard they try,
In comes Sharon Osbourne who is quite kind,
And reassures everyone that they're good at singing in their mind!

Now they have had their competition,
I hope they realise their mission,
Soon they will be turning extremely old,
And everyone wishes we could get a reward
For putting up with them,
I hope it's a pot of gold!

Elliece Worboys (10)
St Leonard's CE Primary School, St Leonards-on-sea

There's A Little Girl Called Annie

There's a little girl called Annie
She went to see her nanny
When she opened the door,
And saw Annie's bold eye
Then she started to cry.

Ryan Mills (11)
St Leonard's CE Primary School, St Leonards-on-sea

The Boy That Got Told Off

I was sitting in the street,
Rubbing my tiny feet.

When I suddenly saw,
A giant Gaw!

It was my mum telling me off,
Because I had a dirty cloth.

William Morrison (11)
St Leonard's CE Primary School, St Leonards-on-sea

Dolphins

D is for dolphins
O is for obviously clever
L is for leaping
P is for playing
H is for healthy
I is for independent
N is for naughty
S is for swimming.

Alice Moye (10)
St Leonard's CE Primary School, St Leonards-on-sea

I Like

I like driving sheep because they go beep, beep
And I like Mr Bean because he eats ice cream.
I like my brother because he says, 'Mother.'

Sean Robinson (11)
St Leonard's CE Primary School, St Leonards-on-sea

Some Mums

Some mums are small,
And some mums are tall,
Some mums are very scary,
And some mums are extremely hairy,
Some mums are merrily sweet
And some mums have stenching feet,
Some mums like to be nice,
And some mums have big headlice,
Some mums are always in a mood,
And some mums are always in the nude,
But my mum can be all of those
And everybody else's mums, who knows.

Daniel Price (11)
St Leonard's CE Primary School, St Leonards-on-sea

How Do Parents Know So Much

Mum, the tree's fallen on the house,
Plant another one then,
Mum the bee's stung me,
Then sting them back.

How do parents know the answer,
To everything?

Dad there's spiders in my bed,
Sleep in your sister's room,
Dad I hurt my leg,
Well kiss it better.

Why do parents know everything?

Hannah Withers (11)
St Leonard's CE Primary School, St Leonards-on-sea

Snow

Snow, snow on the ground,
Dancing and prancing all around,
Comes out of the clouds like beer,
As fast as a deer,
I don't like snowstorms,
So I have to wrap up warm,
My sister got wet,
She got upset.

Annabel Hill (7)
St Margaret's Junior School, Midhurst

My Poem

There was a young man from Leeds,
Who sat down on some beads,
He jumped up high,
And touched the sky,
And landed on some fleas.

Ellie Wood-Crainey (8)
St Margaret's Junior School, Midhurst

My Teacher Thinks . . .

I'm a pupil at St Margaret's School
My teacher thinks I am a fool,
But I don't think I am at all,
Because she really thinks she's cool.

Hamish Petty (8)
St Margaret's Junior School, Midhurst

I Can't Get To Sleep

I've tried counting frogs,
I've tried counting dogs,
But I can't get to sleep,
I need something to eat,
The noise from the dogs is loud,
I wish I was floating on a cloud.

Lydia Marks (7)
St Margaret's Junior School, Midhurst

Snow

Snowflakes, snowflakes everywhere
I caught a snowflake in my hair,
The north wind does blow and we shall have snow,
My sledge goes flying down the hill,
If I get wet I could be ill,
Snow, snow please don't go,
Please have another blow.

Lydia Nethercott-Garabet (7)
St Margaret's Junior School, Midhurst

My Poem

I'm a pupil at St Margaret's School,
And my teacher thinks I'm a fool,
I fell on the floor,
I shut the door,
But I'm not very sure about the rule.

Floss Pearce (7)
St Margaret's Junior School, Midhurst

My School Poem

I'm a pupil at St Margaret's School,
And my teacher thinks I'm a fool,
I blew a bubble,
I got into trouble,
Then I threw the bubbles in the pool.

Mary Hunter (8)
St Margaret's Junior School, Midhurst

Me The Rabbit

Hippity, hoppity, floppedy flip,
My ear looks like a pip,
My nose did a hop,
And looked like a mop,
I gave myself a whippedy dip.

Eliza Ingham (7)
St Margaret's Junior School, Midhurst

A Boy At St Margaret's School

I'm a boy at St Margaret's School,
And my teacher thinks I'm a fool
I was playing in class
She was wearing a mask,
The teacher was trying to look cool.

Tom Condon (8)
St Margaret's Junior School, Midhurst

Whizz, Pop, Bang

I went to a party one day,
And felt really happy to play,
There was a balloon up in the air,
And came down a week today,
It floated down and down,
I was laughing like a clown,
I really like my life,
I felt as sharp as a knife,
I went home for bed,
And cuddled up with Mr Ted,
I felt cosy in bed,
But Mr Ted just fell out of my bed,
In the morning I went to school,
And I was looking like a big fool
But my friends think I'm very cool.

Emily Gunter (7)
St Margaret's Junior School, Midhurst

School

I'm a pupil at St Margaret's School,
My teacher thinks that I'm a fool,
My big teacher
Called me a creature
But I think that I am cool.

Holly Shellard (8)
St Margaret's Junior School, Midhurst

Snow

Sprinkling and twinkling out of the clouds,
Snow falling on the ground,
Swirling and whirling like cotton wool,
Sparkling on the trees like lights shining on them.

Chloe Thomas (7)
St Margaret's Junior School, Midhurst

The Power Of Light

Like a dragon with its wings spread
Breathing out amazing colours of blue and red
Its light wings beating slowly
Its colours are flowing freely
A slender stag stands watching

Standing upon a hilltop grows
It stands watching the rows and rows
The light flickers threatening to leave
Then it spreads its glow across the leaves
Still the stag stands watching

The mountains like dark towers
Trying to destroy the power
Hunters stop hunting a wild mountain boar
They stop and stare
Others then join

The eyes of the stags look like hundreds of amazing jewels
Glinting in the dim light
And then it leaves
One by one the stags go free
Except the first one still stands
Waiting its return

Waiting, waiting
Waiting for evermore.

Ben Pothecary (10)
St Margaret's Junior School, Midhurst

School

I'm a pupil at St Margaret's School,
And my teacher thinks I'm a fool
I play football,
And I'm small,
But I think I'm very cool.

Poppy Frazer (8)
St Margaret's Junior School, Midhurst

The Four Seasons

First comes autumn bringing cool, breezy weather.
The leaves on trees turn the crimson red of a sunset,
The gold of a girl's shining hair,
And the brown of an old oak tree.
You can hear the sound of leaves crunching under foot,
As children play hide-and-seek,
The red, gold and brown leaves beneath their feet.

Next comes winter with cold and snowy weather.
The ground is covered with a beautiful blanket of snow.
The snow so pure, white and it sparkles with magic,
Until it has been trampled through.
The blanket turns brown and it loses its beautiful sparkle,
As the children have snowball fights in it,
The pure white snow loses its magical sparkle.

Then comes spring with wet and stormy weather.
Bringing new flowers and trees.
Little lambs gambol about in fresh green fields,
Then suddenly the April showers come hurtling down.
With a clap of thunder and a flash of lightning,
A ferocious spring storm breaks out,
With tremendous claps of thunder and flashes of lightning.

Last but not least comes summer with hot weather.
New luscious green leaves on the trees,
And new flowers dance and prance
While the summer sun shines on a sapphire lake,
The long grass ripples in the gentle breeze.
While butterflies flutter about,
While the long grass ripples in the summer breeze.

Sarah Gill (11)
St Margaret's Junior School, Midhurst

Pollution

The smoke and dirt,
The folk who hurt this land
Is now never felt by human hand.

The stacking chimneys,
Billowing out fluorescent smoke
Are now just one big joke.

Many places I have been
To see these awful scenes.

We thought we owned the sky.
We thought we owned the ground
But it all came crumbling and tumbling down!

Our end by our own hand is inevitable
Just as inevitable as the end of the poem.

But I will leave you with a thought,
Please take a lesson from what I have taught.

Laurence Bigos (11)
St Margaret's Junior School, Midhurst

Run!

Run, run, run!
There's a murderer on the loose and he's got a laser gun.
He's blowing up buildings just for his own fun.
Striking fear into absolutely everyone,
He's piercing their souls taking out their hearts!
And this is only the start.

He's destroying the planet, taking over the Earth.
He's killing us humans and the animals.
Spreading fire in the forests, spreading fire in the towns,
Making cyclopean weapons, setting off earthquakes.
Dismantling the nations so . . .
Run, run, run!

Travers Murgatroyd (10)
St Margaret's Junior School, Midhurst

The Amazon's Story

I remember when I was young,
Trickling down the mountainside,
Laughing and jumping.
I teemed with fish,
I was a stream,
A beautiful stream,
People lived on my banks,
I was their source,
Their food, their life.
Then I was a river,
A shining river,
More people came,
And formed a town,
Yet still I was their source.
Then I grew slower and wider,
I turned a murky dark brown,
Cities grew on my banks,
Children played and swam in me,
I loved every minute of my life.
Then came the sea,
The wonderful sea,
At last, oh at last,
The wonder of being free!
To move wherever I please.

Catherine Beale (11)
St Margaret's Junior School, Midhurst

Fairyland

I want to go to Fairyland and meet some mythical creatures
I want to go to Fairyland and see some magical features
Those fairy treats with lots of sweets you would certainly never see
Those magical spells and wishing wells,
What a wonderful place it would be!

Joanna Dearden (9)
St Margaret's Junior School, Midhurst

Fire

A grain of light,
A spark, flicker, beautiful picture.
A roaring killer.
Friend or foe can be this light
It's blazing colours of orange and red,
Are braided together with golden yellow.
Like thread woven into material.
The killer's heart is pure evil,
Like a bottle filled with poison
Waiting to be spilled.

The blaze has come from a killer
Now to a beautiful picture.
From the pits of Hell,
To a butterfly dancing in the sky.
But fire is a murderer!
As quickly as the beauty came it is gone.
The butterfly is encased in light.
The butterfly is swallowed by flame.
The blue is licked away by the hellish nightmare.

Fire is like all,
It is born so,
It must die,
Before the flame is blown away,
It flares up one more time and dies.
It will return . . .
Someday, sometime, somewhere . . .
Smouldering earth is all that's left,
Where it once burnt.

George Foster (11)
St Margaret's Junior School, Midhurst

Tragic Trauma

Tragic trauma!
Girls screaming,
Boys pounding,
As the school bus comes along.

Tragic trauma!
Girls late,
It's the boys' fate,
As the school bus comes along.

Tragic trauma!
Hopping onto the bus,
With a lot of fuss,
The school bus is here at last.

Tragic trauma!
The boys are shouting,
The girls are listening,
As the school bus moves along.

Tragic trauma!
Standing on seats,
Ripping all the sheets,
The school bus is reaching the zoo, *wahoo!*

Tragic trauma!
Lions pouncing,
Teachers words pronouncing,
We're here, the zoo, *wahoo!*

Tragic trauma!
A long and tiring trip,
Gotta have a kip,
In bed, in bed.

Joe Shellard (11)
St Margaret's Junior School, Midhurst

The Creature Of Mystery

Surrounded by Misty Mountains,
The wild forest whispering,
A creature drank from a sapphire lake.
Its coat of many colours,
Unseen by mankind,
The colours of heaven,
A watercolour dream.
With hooves of pure white,
Like newly-fallen snow.
Wings, softer then angels,
Pearl-white.
An Arabian horse,
Pegasus-like.
Its eyes are like windows,
They show us its mind.
A book of all knowledge,
From all ages of time.
A mane of shimmering silver,
Fine, like spider's web thread,
Shining like raindrops, a reflection
Spun by the moon.
It lets out a cry,
As soft as a dove,
For the use of freewill
'Save your world'
- Our future in our hands.
Opening its wings, an angel in flight,
Soaring through the velvet of night,
Towards the dark horizon.

Charlotte Vergette (11)
St Margaret's Junior School, Midhurst

The Golden Eye

The moon, my torch light,
My friend, my comfort,
The golden eye in my hand,
Streaming light towards my face,
There's a race against time,
Once the eye stops shining,
The world stops,
I pass the treetops,
The leaves flop,
I stop,
The shining stops,
We stopped,
Silence,
No sound,
We froze . . .

Caitlin gape O'Donnell (10)
St Margaret's Junior School, Midhurst

The Renault

I was walking down the road,
Peaceful and quiet,
But then I saw this car coming,
I immediately started running.
I ran for my life,
As fast as I could,
Then I noticed what car it was,
It was a Renault!
The next thing, I found myself in hospital,
Nothing of my body could move or go,
But I still can't get over it,
Being run over by a Renault!

Izzie Hargreaves (10)
St Margaret's Junior School, Midhurst

The 4 Seasons

What is that I can hear?
Birds singing a merry tune,
Children laughing as free as the wind,
The calm breeze blowing against my face.
Flowers opening their magnificent beaming heads,
Animals begin life seeing a bright world surrounding them,
Spring has arrived yet again!

The summer sun sends light and warmth down,
Giving the earth a healthy glow.
Now, a gentle breeze never comes,
'I need a drink! Quick! Quick! Save me!' Cries the dry land.
Black clouds draw in, the heavens open.
Run for cover, a shelter is needed,
To escape from this summer storm.

Autumn comes with a fierce,
Blowing leaves of different colours,
Scarlet, gold, fawn and ochre,
Crackling crisp beneath our feet.
A swirling ripple of colours,
Covered by frost.
Autumn is nearly gone.

The land is bare,
Quiet and silent in the snow.
The trees sway in the ferocious breeze,
Nothing is there, nothing will grow,
Christmas is near,
Snow is falling,
And soon we will hear spring calling.

Harley Evans (11)
St Margaret's Junior School, Midhurst

Dreams

People dream all the time,
They sometimes think it in a rhyme.
Dreams are your imagined thoughts,
Long or short, dreams can be allsorts.
Dreams take you to far off places,
Where you imagine lots of faces.
Dreams can give you lots of ideas,
Sometimes bring you close to tears.
Dreams can help your imagination,
And fill you with lots of sensation.
Dreams can be lots of fun,
Like winning a race and shouting, 'I've won!'
Dreams can make you feel sad,
Like a dream that is bad.
Dreams can be exciting,
And seem to pass like lightning.
Children dream, adults dream,
Dreams can make you really keen.

Emily Shaw (9)
St Margaret's Junior School, Midhurst

The Sunset On The Beach

The sun was setting on a beautiful day
Behind the lush green hills,
The glistening, shimmering, sparkling sea
In the bay near the house was gold,
With the dim and gorgeous light,
The sun's last rays of warmth and joy were shining on her.
As she sat on her window seat
Basking in its glow.
As it said goodnight and sleep tight
So the moon and its stars could rise again.

Lottie MacCallum (10)
St Margaret's Junior School, Midhurst

Homework

Homework is a boring thing,
I think it should be banned.
Everyone will agree with me,
I think you'll understand.

Every child across the world,
Will think it's a good idea.
Everyday I think of why,
The children always cheer.

Homework can be fun,
But that is very rare.
We sometimes make excuses,
Like, 'It's been eaten by a bear!'

When we get stuck in the middle of a sum,
We usually ask for help,
Our parents say what the answer is
And surely will be help.

Sometimes we can't do our homework,
Because we're doing something else.
Like playing cricket in the courtyard,
Or seeing our auntie, who's Welsh.

Katie Hoolahan (10)
St Margaret's Junior School, Midhurst

The Tree

Trees blow like dancers around the floor.
They drift around and scatter their leaves.
Their branches wave like the sea.
Their branches swoop up and down.
Their pine cones drop like snow falling to the ground.
Their roots look like they go on forever.
When it is a windy day the tree does not stop waving,
But when it is a nice day it looks like the tree is asleep.

Kai Horne (10)
St Margaret's Junior School, Midhurst

Christmas

We love Christmas,
It's the best time of year.
Presents and chocolate, our favourite!
Getting together with our families,
And having lots of fun.

When the snow falls,
When it's getting late,
The only light is from a fireplace.
When the fire goes out,
When we go to bed,
He takes his chance.

When no one's about,
He creeps out, onto his sleigh,
With the presents loaded,
And the reindeer attached,
He sails off into the darkness.

He jumps down the chimneys,
He eats the mince pies,
He gives his reindeer carrots,
And the children a big surprise,
From house to house he moves,
Filling stockings and eating food.

When morning comes,
The snow is still white,
Children wake up in great delight.
Their stockings are full,
Presents everywhere,
Santa Claus has been this year.

Katie Hill   (10)
St Margaret's Junior School, Midhurst

The British Lion

T he British Lions rock!
H ey, what a try
E very game they win.

B ang, go the tackles
R ucking is their speciality
I t simply astonishes me
T hey'll muller any team
I watch them in the stands
S o powerful in their pack.
H yne's loves getting points.

L ingering on the wing is Williams.
I ncoming ball; he catches.
O ff he goes!
N ew on the pitch;

Williams scores a fabulous try!

William Proud (10)
St Margaret's Junior School, Midhurst

Half-Term

Half-term is the best time of year,
It gives me time to sit down and watch Top Gear.
It's a nice long satisfied rest,
But there's still my little sister who's a big pest.
I sometimes go out to see some friends,
I'm having such a great time that
I forgot about when half-term ends.
The thought of school is a terrible thing,
The thought of the first day when you hear your alarm clock ring,
But the worst thing is not breaking a bone,
It's going back to school, which takes nerves of stone.

William Soulsby (10)
St Margaret's Junior School, Midhurst

Happiness

Happiness is daffodils swaying in the breeze,
It's sweet, sweet honey straight from the bees,
Happiness is sunlight beaming on my head,
Happiness is wrapping up in a cosy warm bed.

Happiness is music coming from a drum,
Like a big hug from my mum,
Like a rainbow over my head,
Like a hug from my ted.

Happiness is a sandy beach, on which I comfortably lie,
Happiness is a hard crunchy pie,
Happiness is a dewdrop settling down,
Happiness is a big present my mum got from town.

Happiness is snow melting away
Happiness is going out to play
Happiness is having lots of friends,
Happiness is talking about current trends.

Kris Carr (10)
St Margaret's Junior School, Midhurst

Reading

I've known how to read,
Since I was a little girl.
Mrs Benzing said you couldn't do anything,
If you don't know how to read.
As I got older I've read harder books,
And apparently I've extended my vocabulary.
Reading isn't my thing,
But I sometimes like to read.
I think I will read for the rest of my life.

Natalie Wood-Crainey (10)
St Margaret's Junior School, Midhurst

Motor Engines

Engines can be small,
Engines can be big,
Engines can be powerful,
Engines can be weak.
There are many types of engines,
Car engines,
Aeroplane engines,
Motorbike engines.
From moped engines,
To jet engines.
Engines can be loud,
Engines can be quiet,
Engines can be electric,
Engines can run on oils.
Engines can pollute,
Some engines don't pollute.
And without motor engines,
There wouldn't be power,
Or electricity.
And without electricity,
There wouldn't be computers,
Oh no!

Tristan Le Butt (10)
St Margaret's Junior School, Midhurst

Anger

Anger is a fierce lion, ready to pounce,
Anger is a mammoth thundering through your brain,
Anger is a fire burning in your eyes,
Anger is a looming, booming storm,
A gigantic blizzard of poisonous words,
Pouring out to hurt.

Adam Cooke (10)
St Margaret's Junior School, Midhurst

Minty The Pony

Minty is a little horse
Almost too small for me to ride
No one can catch her, of course
Because she absolutely loves to hide.

Her canter is fast
But she is reasonably sensible
She never comes last
But she really loves to pull.

She really tries to buck
She is terribly scary
But animals do have some luck
Even Buster the dog, who is very hairy.

Minty enjoys jumping
She sometimes goes too far
The ground she does like jumping
It almost goes to the gate's bar.

Minty is a welsh mountain pony
Able to carry heavy loads
She is not fat. She is bony.
She never likes going on roads.

Martha Campolmi (10)
St Margaret's Junior School, Midhurst

Cricket

C ricket is a fun, cool sport
R unning is good for cricket
I like bowling in cricket
C ricket is cool
K ids like cricket
E veryone will play,
'T il night has come.

William Hopper (9)
St Margaret's Junior School, Midhurst

Anger

Anger is red, immediately from your mind,
It is curly and frustrating as if you were dead.
Anger is a fist clutching itself tight.
As if there was a dagger straight through your head.

Anger is a gun firing from the sky,
Just like you had a bullet right in your eye.
You slam doors behind you as if you were mad.
It is nothing but darkness, not like being glad.

Angus Petty (10)
St Margaret's Junior School, Midhurst

Summer

S ummer is coming,
U mbrellas not needed,
M ost people at the beach,
M ost people drinking water,
E ric is going swimming,
R icky is going fishing.

Alice Parry (8)
St Margaret's Junior School, Midhurst

Rugby

R ugby is cool
U mbrellas in the crowd,
G oal posts covered in mud,
B alls everywhere,
Y ou will get muddy.

Katie Greaves (9)
St Margaret's Junior School, Midhurst

Snow

Sprinkling and twinkling out of the clouds,
I like to throw snowballs, but was not allowed,
The snow is crunchy and deep under my feet,
My sledge goes flying down the hill,
I get wet, I could be ill,
I get cold, but I don't care,
I like to make angels in the air.

Harriet Shaw (8)
St Margaret's Junior School, Midhurst

School

I'm a pupil at St Margaret's School,
And my teacher thinks I'm a fool,
I sat on my chair
My teacher let out a glare,
It's not fair.

Alice Menon (8)
St Margaret's Junior School, Midhurst

Boats

B ig or small, skimming the water
O ff they sail over the horizon
A lways lots of them gliding around
T rying to be careful not to hit a ferry
S uper and fast is what I think boats are.

William Harrison (9)
St Margaret's Junior School, Midhurst

Fun In The Sun

Down on the beach
On a sunny day
Lots of children
Run and play
Making sandcastles
With a bucket and spade
All different shapes and sizes
Children swimming in
The open sea
Kites flying high
In the sky
People sunbathing
On the sand
Jet skis whizzing
Up and down
Men in their fishing boats
Casting our their lines
Children playing
Their favourite games
Eating ice cream
To cool them down
Sailing boats moving
Slowly in the breeze
While speedboats
Are whizzing around
And making waves.

Josh Read (10)
St Margaret's Junior School, Midhurst

Anger

Anger is a giant storming through the town,
Anger is a cold, wet, stormy day when you can't go out to play,
Anger is a tightness inside when people exclude you
                              from their games.

Scarlett Abraham (10)
St Margaret's Junior School, Midhurst

Joy

Joy is splashing about in a sparkling cold river in the sunlight.
Joy is a sprinkling bright day at the silvery sandy beach.
Joy is winning races on sports' day and making it
                                        to the finish line first.
Joy is galloping horses in their paddock with flowing
                                        black and brown manes.
Joy is seeing your family's smiles at Christmas as they open presents.

Sophie Forsyth (9)
St Margaret's Junior School, Midhurst

Kate And Her Mate

There was a young girl called Kate,
Who went to see her mate,
They went for a walk,
And started to talk,
So when they got home, they were late.

Annabel Pope (9)
St Margaret's Junior School, Midhurst

Tiger

T hrough the jungle prowls a tiger
I n its eyes are flames of fire
G rowling noises roam the treetops
E choing the pounding from the tiger's paws
R ain taps on the orange and black coat of the jungle king.

Freya Lawes (8)
St Margaret's Junior School, Midhurst

The Day I Nibbled My Nail Off

Once I was nibbling my nail,
When I looked at it it was very frail,
I bit once more and off fell my nail onto the floor!

My mum came to see what was the matter
I said my nail had come off
When I was having it for a quick scoff
After tea which was cod in batter
I went to bed with a spinning head.

Oliver Ingham (10)
St Margaret's Junior School, Midhurst

Thrushes

From a nest within
The berry bush I heard a noise,
It was a cracking noise.
I peered in the bush
And saw six beautiful baby thrushes
Chirping their first chirp
And what a lovely sound it was.
I thought what a delight to see such a lovely sight.

Ollie Hallt (10)
St Margaret's Junior School, Midhurst

A Limerick

There once was a Scotsman called Jock
Who felt like becoming a Roman
He set off for Rome
But soon rushed back home
'Cos his toga looked like a frock.

Gregory Ions (9)
St Margaret's Junior School, Midhurst

The Beach

Golden, yellow and white,
Are the colours of the tingling sand
As it slips through my toes,
And across my hand.

Blue, green and aqua,
Are the colours of the peaceful sea,
Whispering and foaming,
As it creeps towards me.

Yellow, red and orange,
Are the colours of the blazing sun,
As it settles heat upon me,
And I'm having lots of fun.

Shrieks, yells and laughter,
Echo round the bay,
Children licking ice creams,
Squealing as they play.

Annabel Atkins (10)
St Margaret's Junior School, Midhurst

My Pony

Harvey is my pony,
His height is twelve hands three
And his coat is golden brown
He could jump as high as me.

In cross country,
We gallop around the course
Trying to get a clear round
Once we did come first!

We are not the best at dressage,
But we passed the test
Last time when we cantered
We went over the line.

Katie Griffiths (9)
St Margaret's Junior School, Midhurst

Weather

At last, at last it's May
Oh no the sky is grey!
I look up to see the cloud
I shout so very loud.
'Oh no I hate the rain
It is a real pain!'
At last out comes the sun
Now I can have some fun
A quick dip in the pool
Before I go to school
What's that I hear you say?
Wake up it's another day?
A dream it must have been
It's snowing!

Harriet Hind (10)
St Margaret's Junior School, Midhurst

My Dog

My dog is an angel,
Put upon this Earth,
Like a shooting star she fell,
Into my life after her birth.

She is a golden-ginger colour,
Glowing in the sun,
My cat looks at her and begins to purr,
She delights my mum.

She is as gentle as a mouse,
As sweet as a lamb,
She makes our house,
As sweet as jam.

Amy Marks (10)
St Margaret's Junior School, Midhurst

Colour

When the clouds are grey,
I just sit and prey,
That the wind will blow them away.

When the sky is blue,
I think it through,
Hoping that I can play with you.

The colour of pink,
Just makes me think,
How I love to wink.

When I see brown,
I think of a clown,
And I jump up and down.

When I see white,
I see the sight of a bright light,
And I get a fright.

When I see red,
I have a very sore head,
And I want my bed.

When I see green,
I love to clean,
And I think of a lovely scene.

When I see gold,
I feel cold,
And I look at the things that are old.

When I see yellow,
I love to bellow,
Just like a fellow.

Emily Hallt (10)
St Margaret's Junior School, Midhurst

Flame

Fire is a perilous tool of major destruction,
It disperses rapidly, tossing wafts of billowing smoke high above.
It creeps into cracks of even a minute size,
The smoke it produces is thick and foggy.
The fire, twisting and turning, gobbling everything in its path.

Fire, friend or foe,
Fire can be as beneficial as you, you know.
It whips up a dinner; it keeps your toes warm,
Private junk can be burnt; it gives light in a storm.
For this do not try and avoid it so.

Fire is a spectacular sight,
It is usually made up of oranges and reds,
But can have a small portion of yellow.
Blue and white are the hottest of all,
And by far the most dangerous brand,
You have to be careful,
For everybody's brains are not always switched on,
And are often on a different land.

Erin Murgatroyd (9)
St Margaret's Junior School, Midhurst

Anger

Anger is the shout of a giant,
Anger is a boom of thunder,
Anger strikes like lightning,
Anger is a dog's growl,
Anger is hot like the desert's sun,
Anger is a volcano erupting,
Anger is a storm inside you,
Anger is as red as blood.

Lottie Marchant (10)
St Margaret's Junior School, Midhurst

The Zebra

The friendly zebra all black and white,
I love with all my heart,
Stripes like lines,
That swirl like vines,
I will soon find,
The zebra is kind.

On the safari I go,
The zebra waits very low,
Hiding from the human eye,
Because it is very shy,
A glimpse of him I see,
Dashing in-between the trees.

It has made my day,
To see him on his way,
My love will never end,
He is my favourite friend,
Until the very end.

Philippa Bridger (10)
St Margaret's Junior School, Midhurst

A Cold And Frosty Day

On a cold and frosty day,
My feet get very cold,
I fear I might get frostbite,
When it's very cold.

Damp and frosty,
Cold and wet,
My body freezes,
My brain won't set.

Oh how I hate the cold,
For my nose is glowing red,
My fingertips are numb,
I'm dreaming of my warm bed.

Lizzie Farrington (9)
St Margaret's Junior School, Midhurst

I Like Science

First we come to chemistry,
Chemistry is cool!
There's the chemicals that bubble
As you sit on the high stool.
There are the test tubes in the racks,
There are the beakers too,
If you mix the right chemicals
They'll make you go blue,
We're heating up the test tubes, wait, I heard a clang,
Bang!

Next comes physics,
Physics is fantastic,
I like to make robots,
Made with metal wood and plastic.
You put the batteries in the robots,
Which supply it with power,
I only hope my next robot,
Is powered for more than an hour
I suddenly noticed, my robot started to frown,
Help! He's burnt the school down!

Lastly comes biology,
Biology is bliss,
I put on my black wellies
And go and look at fish.
I go and look at frogs and toads,
I do it every day,
In rain and snow and sun and wind,
Whatever, come what may,
Through this muddy puddle I am sploshing,
Whoops, Mum, I think I've got some washing.

Joseph Tupper (9)
St Margaret's Junior School, Midhurst

A Glittery Morning

The curtains had hidden the white, white world,
As the shiny flakes swirled and twirled,
Little stars fell from the sky,
Dancing down then up until, they die.

No more grass, no more green,
No red roofs anywhere to be seen,
Only lumps and bumps hiding all that's known,
Even the birds seen to have flown.

Far, far away children are sledding and sliding,
Squealing and screaming, calling and colliding,
Snowballs fly in cold, cold faces,
Fingers freeze as flakes cover all traces.

Harry Kwok (9)
Skippers Hill Manor Preparatory School, Mayfield

Snow, Snow

Snow, snow
Where did you go?
Woke up this morning
And you were gone

Snow, snow
Where did you go?
Was it because the
Sun had shone?

Snow, snow
That sparkled so bright
Hope to see you
Tomorrow night.

Douglas Cook (10)
Skippers Hill Manor Preparatory School, Mayfield

Snowy

Hooray it's snowing I will need a good breakfast today.
I gulp it down and put on
My hat and coat and tumble outside.
I stop to catch my breath.
There is an eerie silence,
Snowflakes floating in the winter breeze.
They are cold and icy,
But light as a feather.
The sun is shining and
The snow glistens and is
Bright and white.
I race back inside
And phone a friend
And say, 'Want a snow fight?'
I grab the snow and squeeze
It tight and get ready for
My fight.

Luke Lyons (9)
Skippers Hill Manor Preparatory School, Mayfield

Snowy Ride

The icy snow shone and sparkled like Fairy dust
The soft beauty made everything look so lovely
But then a big

Gust!

We knew we had to go on in the car we must
I was sad my sister wasn't here, it was too dangerous,
And I suppose she would have fussed
Suddenly
A big blizzard hit us, 'Don't worry it's just a blizzard,'
Said my mum.

Amelia Voke (9)
Skippers Hill Manor Preparatory School, Mayfield

I Hate Shopping

I hate shopping
Don't know what it might be
My brother loves the supermarket
But shopping is not for me

We do shopping every week
Normally at the weekend
I have got a thing with shopping
It drives me round the bend

Cabbages and carrots
Silly paper cards
Whenever we go shopping
I lock myself in the car!

David Parker (9)
Skippers Hill Manor Preparatory School, Mayfield

The Snow Nightmare

Shivering in the wind of the snowy night
I catch a snowflake on my tongue and make it into a game of fun.

Big fat snowflakes falling fast from the enormous winter sky
Like freezing white feathers falling from an injured bird.

The flakes are falling fast now swirling me in a snowstorm of icy-cold.
Then suddenly I get lifted off my feet and get sent falling down
Through the freezing cold air into my bed where I wake to find
That it was all just a bad dream.

Louis Catliff (9)
Skippers Hill Manor Preparatory School, Mayfield

My Snowy Poem

Snow! Snow!
Everywhere
Every corner
Every square
Icy flakes falling everywhere.

Soft beauty everywhere
Quietly piling the square
Blizzards coming down the road
Quick before they load.

Snow is cold
Icy-cold
Freezing icy flakes
Snowballs being thrown
Down the road
Quick! Quick!
Escape!

Samantha Hedley (10)
Skippers Hill Manor Preparatory School, Mayfield

The Snow Queen

Snow
Is white
In sunlight
Bright and fluffy,
Soft and fun. But when
Blizzard blows the fun goes
And the Snow Queen comes out
To play.

Alec Pultr (10)
Skippers Hill Manor Preparatory School, Mayfield

Snow

The
Dazzling
White snow
Sitting on the tops
Of trees making them shiver and shine in the winter sun,
Covering up the snowmen with its snowy blanket,
Icy-cold icicles hanging from a frozen roof,
Sparkling snowflakes falling in the
Freezing blizzard, children having snowball fights
Behind snowy walls, children sledding down great snowy hills,
The snowflakes falling into ominous shapes,
Shining shimmering
Sparkling snow
Falling from
The sky.

Angus Plummer (10)
Skippers Hill Manor Preparatory School, Mayfield

Octopus

Splashing, splishing
Hiding under rocks
Making noises
Sliding around
Tricking other creatures
Pretending to be
Jellyfish cuddled
Up together
Later octopus had
Scared all the creatures.
Away.

Alex Wood (7)
Skippers Hill Manor Preparatory School, Mayfield

Skiing

At the top of the slope waiting, waiting.
I start long turns one, two, three, four
I see a jump. Small turns, quick turn
Faster and faster. Suddenly a boarder
Sneaks past. Faster straight faster
Very fast. Now the jumps close
Almost there. *Click-clack*
Then in the air lifting
Lifting
Falling, falling!
Panic! Falling very fast close to the snow 3, 2, 1
Crash
Frozen in deep powder getting very cold down my neck
Around my toes and nose.
Frozen to the spot.

Rory Ellis (10)
Skippers Hill Manor Preparatory School, Mayfield

Snow, Snow, Snow

Snow is wet
   Snow is soggy
      Snow is fun
         Snow is foggy
Snow is bright
   Snow is clear
      Snow is fun
         Snow is here
Snow is white
   Snow is clean
      Snow is bad
         Snow is mean.

Bradley Wheeler (10)
Skippers Hill Manor Preparatory School, Mayfield

Snowy Days

I woke up at 7.30am
Then I ran downstairs I grabbed
My coat, my hat, scarf, boots
I ran outside my feet dipped
In that nice soft beauty of whiteness

Icy flakes tapped on my head
I looked up at the sky, the blizzard
Got harder and harder, but I still
Saw the glitter of sun.
In the distance I saw white polar beasts.

Then when the day got on, the blizzard
Stopped the sun came out,
Then the snow was gone.
But I can still smell the snow,
I'm dreaming all alone again.

Rosie Barrett (10)
Skippers Hill Manor Preparatory School, Mayfield

The Bed Boat

I sail along dreaming my dreams,
Below the deck is where I sleep upon the floor.
The blue carpet is the sea,
The flying sail is my duvet.
I lean over the headboard watching the choppy sea.

The dingy following along behind is my dressing table stool.
The wind whistling past my ear.
My fellow passenger, my bear, enjoying the warmth of my cuddle.

Sophie Grant (11)
Skippers Hill Manor Preparatory School, Mayfield

My Sister

My sister is really mean,
I hate her.
Yesterday she took the front seat of the car,
Even though it was my day,
I hate her.
The day before that she ruined my school dress,
I hate her.
Three days ago she got me sent to my room for nothing,
Well, I only kicked her.
I hate her.
Four days ago she took all my sweets and showed
                         my mum my secret crisp store.
I hate her.
My mum says deep down I really love her.
I don't think it's true.
But this morning she gave me two Refreshers.
Maybe she isn't so bad after all . . .

Jenny Shepherd (9)
Skippers Hill Manor Preparatory School, Mayfield

Brothers And Sisters

Why are brothers so black and boring?
Why are sisters so silly and stupid?
Why is the middle one always left out?
        It's me!
        It's me!
What's wrong with me?

Brothers get the best.
Sisters get the sandpits.
Why is the middle one always left out?
        It's me!
        It's me!
Somebody tell me what's wrong with me!

Emily Webb (9)
Skippers Hill Manor Preparatory School, Mayfield

If Only I Was A Bird

The beautiful song of a bird,
The mighty speed of a bird,
If only I was a bird.

The colourful feathers of a bird,
The razor-sharp beak of a bird,
If only I was a bird.

The sparkly eyes of a bird,
The sharp claws of a bird,
If only I was a bird.

The daily food from a human for a bird,
The free skies for a bird,
If only I was a bird.

The waviness of the tree for a bird,
The constructive ability of a bird,
If only I was a bird.

The big cuddly mum of a bird,
The warm nest of a bird,
If only I was a bird.

I want to be a bird!

Alexander Sparrow (8)
Skippers Hill Manor Preparatory School, Mayfield

The Squishy Squid

The slippery squabbling squid.
    Squabbling through slippery sea.
The squid was squishy and squashy and slippery.
    It squelched and slipped and squabbled.
Through the slippery slimy cold wet sea.

Marella Reis (8)
Skippers Hill Manor Preparatory School, Mayfield

Jellyfish

Splishing, splashing
Hiding under rocks.

Tripping, flipping
Stinging other fish.

Sniffing, fliffing
Hunting for their dinner.

Puffing, bluffing
Running from each other.

Ben Poon (8)
Skippers Hill Manor Preparatory School, Mayfield

Jellyfish

Jellyfish squabble
Jellyfish wobble
Jellyfish don't think
That they are any trouble.

Jellyfish are pink
Jellyfish stink
I wish this jellyfish would shrink.

Katherine Sparrow (7)
Skippers Hill Manor Preparatory School, Mayfield

Snow And Ice

Snow falls as ice,
Winds as cold as blizzards,
Ice shines in the light,
Kids sledging in the frosty snow,
Snowmen proud to stand,
Water freezes to ice,
Ice glitters like a crystal,
Creatures wander in the snow.

Jason Tsang (10)
Skippers Hill Manor Preparatory School, Mayfield

Homework

Homework is a monster ready to pounce into your bag,
Changing your books.

Homework is a snake swallowing you whole
Until you've done your science prep.

Latin and French demons jump from classrooms
Giving you more and more foreign nonsense.

Voices come from nowhere telling you to do your history
Giving you long lectures on rebellions.

Drama ghosts and singers are rehearsing Romeo and Juliet
And telling you to learn your lines or else . . . !

But now it is home time and I've got so many preps:
An essay on acids,
Three sheets on French.
Four sheets on Latin.
A comprehension on rebellions
And learn my lines.

I'm home!
'Have you got any prep?' says Mum.
Voice of the television reaches my ears,
In a trance I sit on the sofa.
The television monster speaks.
My Clarinet calls to be practised,
My brother is playing with his cars
It's not fair!

Homework is ruining my life!

Elizabeth Atkinson (10)
Skippers Hill Manor Preparatory School, Mayfield

The Mountain

At the top of the mountain,
The snow was fresh and new,
Before I started skiing,
I stopped to admire the view.

Although the sun was shining,
The air was freezing cold,
The snow that was beneath me,
Shone up at me like gold.

The snow was fast and icy,
As I skied off the mountain,
I screeched to a halt at the bottom,
And the snow sprayed up like a fountain!

Sophie Pegram Heron (9)
Skippers Hill Manor Preparatory School, Mayfield

Here Comes The Snow

I can smell the snow
Look, look here it comes
In big and small
Icy
Flakes
There's lots of
Flat flakes
Soft flakes
Icy flakes
All in dazzling white shiny
And
Bright.

Natasha Howie (10)
Skippers Hill Manor Preparatory School, Mayfield

The Cataract At Lodore

(An alternative verse to the poem by Robert Southey)

Then suddenly falling and
Slipping and tumbling and striking
And diving and descending and
Plummeting and plunging and
Smashing and exploding and
Crashing and bashing and
Bubbling and foaming and
Fizzing.

Then quietening and calming
And calming and clearing and
Deepening and reflecting and
Shining and rippling and ceasing
And drooling and pooling and

Still . . .

Very still.

James Wood (9)
Skippers Hill Manor Preparatory School, Mayfield